ULTRA HIGH FIDELITY
Dot
Lowery Music &
Lyresong Music
BMI
Time 2:32
BYE BYE, SILLY
(Harry Karras)
THE SWINGING
MEDALLIONS
3-65
DOT RECORDS, INC., HOLLYWOOD, CALIFORNIA • A DIVISION O

SAVE THE LAST DANCE FOR ME

A LOVE STORY OF THE SHAG AND THE SOCIETY OF STRANDERS

Phil Sawyer and Tom Poland

The University of South Carolina Press

© 2012 University of South Carolina

Published by the University of South Carolina Press
Columbia, South Carolina 29208

www.sc.edu/uscpress

Manufactured in the United States of America

21 20 19 18 17 16 15 14 13 12   10 9 8 7 6 5 4 3 2 1

Library of Congress Cataloging-in-Publication Data

Sawyer, Phil.
Save the last dance for me : a love story of the shag and
the society of stranders / Phil Sawyer, Tom Poland.
p. cm.
Includes index.
ISBN 978-1-61117-087-0 (hardback)—ISBN 978-1-61117-088-7 (pbk)
1. Shag (Dance)—History. 2. Shag (Dance)—South Carolina—History.
3. South Carolina—Social life and customs. I. Poland, Thomas M., 1949–
II. Title.
GV1796.S5S28 2012
793.3'3—DC23   2012011628

This book was printed on a recycled paper with
30 percent postconsumer waste content.

To Miss Chick
and
To the Music Man—Robert Anthony Plant

The Music Walked Out of Clarksdale

The Society of Stranders was built from serendipity.

Gene "Swink" Laughter

Contents

SHAG: SOUTH CAROLINA'S STATE DANCE

Proud shaggers and S.O.S. members watch Governor Dick Riley
make the shag South Carolina's official state dance April 10, 1984,
enacting Representative Bubber Snow's bill.

Courtesy of Phil Sawyer.

Acknowledgments

We wish to thank Joan Bassett, Frank Beacham, Susie Beaver, Judy and Wayne Bennett, Fat Harold Bessent, Jimmy Buffkin, Al and M. G. Cain, Donna Cardwell, Vicki Chaffin, Jim Dodson, Brendan Greaves, Cal Harrison, Kay Hatcher, Sarah Hettich, Noel Hill, Historic Columbia Foundation and Charley Holtzclaw, John Hook, Dorothy Jarrett, Linda (Burress) Joyce, Joan Kimbro, Amy Kinard, Gene "Swink" Laughter, Kay Maddox, Mike Marr, Bosie Martin Technical Support, Charlotte Moore, Joan Moore, Jan Morris, Milford Powell, Bonnie Rhodes, James Salem, David Sessoms, Vicki Sewell, Ken Smith, John "Bubber" Snow, Bryant and Vanessa Stephens, Buffy Stewart, Helen Still, Becky Stowe, Ellen Taylor, Larry Taylor, Michael C. Taylor, Jack Thompson, Chris Toenes, Pam Traugott, Donna Tuthill, Carolyn Vaughan, Donnie Way, Jeff Wilkinson and the *State,* and Peggy Ann Wrenn.

We also owe a debt to the *Carefree Times* advertising manager, Janet Harold, and the *Carefree Times* editor, Mike Payne.

Past chairmen of the Association of Carolina Shag Clubs Board of Advisers include Ron Whisenant, Ken Hudspeth, Phil Sawyer, Bob Wood, Joe McGee, Mike Rink, Murl Augustine, Judy Vick and Ken Akin.

Past chairmen of the Society of Stranders Board of Directors include Larry Taylor, Bob Wood, Donnie Way, Hector Pfeifer, and Helen Still, and the past president, now president emeritus, is Phil Sawyer.

Special thanks go to Judy Vick and Hector Phifer for encouraging Phil Sawyer to tell the story behind the shag, S.O.S., and South Carolina's state dance. We also want to thank Speedy and Edith Lewis for exceptionally gracious hospitality over the years.

In conclusion we acknowledge club owners, deejays, shag clubs, and all the shaggers out there.

Society of Stranders Officers and Board of Directors

Association of Carolina Shag Clubs
Board of Advisers

Ken Akin, *Chairman*
John Reynolds, *Vice Chairman*
Sonny Brown, *Secretary*
Allen Henry, *Treasurer*
Judy Vick, *Past Chairman*

Prologue

Footprints in the Sand

It's impossible to pinpoint the moment dancing surfaced as part of human culture, but it goes back as far as prehistoric times. Dancing leaves no artifacts, and footprints in the sand prove fleeting. Still, rock paintings indicate that communal dancing goes back nine thousand years. Whether done in tribute to ancient gods, to celebrate abundant crops, or for sheer joy, dancing is ingrained in our DNA.

It should come as no surprise, then, that a group celebrates dancing's joy with the fervor of a religious movement out to convert others. The Society of Stranders (S.O.S.) describes itself as a "cult." The S.O.S. is devoted to that dance of grace associated with beaches, cold beer, beach music, and good times: the shag. In religious-like pilgrimages the S.O.S. migrates winter, spring, and fall to its holy ground, a place once known as Ocean Drive.

In the early 1980s the S.O.S. created a newsletter, *Carefree Times*. From it comes a trove of information that gives this book much of its richness and depth. Shagging is a carefree life, a fine southern life. As T. Edward Nickens wrote in *Smithsonian*, "Down here, the shag is a dance, as old-time Southern as pouring salted peanuts into a sweating bottle of 'co-cola.'"

FOOTPRINTS IN THE SAND

Rhythm and blues found a path to the beach, and beach music
resulted—that soulful music that led to the shag, endless summers,
perpetual youth, romance, and everlasting friendships.

Photograph by Sarah Hettich.

Today thousands return to North Myrtle Beach in the fall, winter, and spring to shag and share good times and memories. Dancers come from all points of the compass, from all walks of life. Onetime exiles, they migrate to their homeland.

The story of the shag and the Society of Stranders is rich with South and North Carolina connections. It sheds light on how the shag became the official dance of both states and how a group who reveres its youthful dance refused to let it die.

The shag is a dance with a pedigree. Around 1903 on an island near Charleston, blacks performed a mesmerizing dance. Mainland blacks adopted it, and Charleston bequeathed its name to this dance of swaying arms, fast feet, kicks, and hops. By 1913 the Charleston had hit nightclubs in Harlem. It spread from New York across the country and ruled the Roaring Twenties—a symbol of the era's daring restlessness.

As flappers pranced through the Roaring Twenties and as Americans cut loose in speakeasies, it was a time for outrageous behavior. The Charleston could be danced alone, with a partner, or in a group. The Charleston spawned the Lindy Hop, jitterbug's fraternal twin.

DOIN' THE CHARLESTON

Around 1903 black people kicked up their heels on an island near Charleston. Dancers on the mainland took it up, and by 1913 it had spread across the nation.

Photograph courtesy of Wikimedia Commons.

At first the Lindy Hop was the province of Harlem's black dancers. During the 1930s the lines defining dances blurred as people innovated steps and music changed. Lindy devotees broke rank: one group stayed conservative, keeping its feet on the floor; the other group favored gravity-defying steps and lifting partners high above the floor. The shag would evolve from the conservative group.

In 1936 during this golden era of dance, awestruck University of South Carolina students watched young blacks in Columbia dance at Fat Sam's Big Apple Night Club. Integration was a quarter-century away, and whites and blacks were supposed to keep a distance between them. The students forbade to dance could, however, watch from the balcony.

Fascinated with the dance's footwork—steps as old as Africa—they danced it at the Myrtle Beach Pavilion. Like the Charleston, the Big Apple (a group circle dance) spread to New York City, and by December 1937 the Big Apple dance craze had swept the nation. South Carolina was writing chapters in dance history and forging a strong connection with jazz. Yet more history, however, was to come.

The shag would evolve—a great river fed by cultural tributaries involving music, agents of change, and stubborn ways. Mainstream radio stations of the 1940s South, for instance, would not play black music, and black bands could not play white clubs. Twisting radio dials all night would not turn up this body-moving music. Wailing saxophones and sultry lyrics, however, found an audience in Ocean Drive and Carolina Beach, and the shag evolved from the cross-pollination of black music and late 1940s, early 1950s white youth—a perfect union.

The shag was to be "a cool sip of charcoal-filtered whiskey" to hip, easy-going beach cats who slowed the dance tempo. Their feet stayed close to the floor, and dancing on the beach gave the moves a cool, unhurried identity, "shagging." Slowing the pace made sense. Dancing as sweat pours off you isn't cool.

The shag was *the* dance along the Grand Strand in the late 1940s and early 1950s—a memorable time of classic cars, ice cream sodas, rhythm and blues, cold beer, and nights afire with love. Many would look back on this golden era as the apex of youth and romance.

It was a glamorous, chivalrous time. As evening fell, the lights of open-air pavilions beckoned. As gleaming lines of surf broke outside pavilions and clubs, couples danced. Neon Wurlitzers and Rock-Olas gobbled change. Shaggers danced along the leading edge of a pop-culture revolution in places indelibly etched in memories: the Myrtle Beach Pavilion, Sonny's Pavilion, Spivey's, Roberts Pavilion, and cramped "jump joints."

Ocean Drive and its stars assumed iconic stature. Lifeguards were bronzed gods. Women were sun-kissed "peaches" to be plucked by men with perfect dance-floor cool. There was nothing like an evening of club hopping, and the shabbier those clubs were, the better.

Just as the shag culture seemed poised to explode across the country, two calamities stopped the dancing. Both, you could say, involved the Atlantic Ocean. Suddenly shagging seemed relegated to footprints in the sand, a footnote to fleeting dance cultures such as the Charleston, the Big Apple, and the jitterbug. A determined effort, however, saved the dance and, later, the Society of Stranders. Here, then, are their intertwined stories.

The shag's saga varies as much of its story is passed down by word of mouth. Beach music historian John Hook addressed this fact: "What folks know and what they assume are different. The institutionalization of the shag culture in the last 30 years is a dramatic departure from the way it was prior to [hurricane] Hazel."

The Society of Stranders' story varies also. Ellen Taylor, shagger and shag instructor, understands the dissonance: "People have their very own story and interpretation of the beginning of S.O.S. We all have our own stories."

Highs, lows, the blues, blacks, whites, race relations, memorable characters, music, disasters, dance, and a self-professed cult—they're all here. Our story reveals how people embraced change as never before, and it speaks with reverence of a place veiled in mystique, Ocean Drive.

Shagging relives the dream. Footprints in the sand will fade. Memories of shagging at O.D. will not.

1

Dancing along the Coast

With three quarters in his pocket and courage in his heart, a country boy from Salley, South Carolina, dared to step onto the dance floor at Roberts Pavilion with a girl one summer night in 1945. He had spent a week at Ocean Drive (O.D.) pining for a chance to dance. Tonight would be his last night at O.D. for a year, and so far he had just watched couples dancing every night. And the watching? It was getting old.

Unaware that beach bums lived by a code, he asked a girl to dance, and onto the floor they stepped—a faux pas. The couple dancing surrendered the floor to them and tossed pennies their way, a put-down, but the country boy didn't know that. He spent the rest of the year thinking he was a dancer of distinction.

The blissful country boy was unaware of the truth, and he wasn't alone. Many dancers had no idea how the music and dance they loved so much had come to be. The story goes way back.

IT WAS JUNE 21, 1945. One of World War II's longest and bloodiest battles, Okinawa, ended. The final acts of World War II were playing out, and war-weary parents welcomed the news. As they watched events in Europe and the Pacific with unprecedented interest, their youths (the term "teenager" was not yet in vogue) had other matters in mind.

Summer 1945 in South Carolina began the day the battle of Okinawa ended. The beach season was under way, and teens coming to the Grand Strand had time to burn. Milling about and listening to music, they killed a lot of time, and they danced—a lot. In the process they were laying the cornerstone for a new culture and in time a cult.

That same year music was changing. *Billboard* declared that swing was falling out of vogue as big bands gave way to vocalists. Meanwhile down in Mississippi the haunting, bluesy music of the common man, the music of everyman, leaped from person to person like wildfire. From jukebox to jump joint the sparks blazed up. Jump joints, simple places with concrete floors, roofs, and jukeboxes, provided the music that shag would grow from, but when?

Want to start a spirited conversation? Ask a group of shaggers how and when the shag began. You'll get plenty of action. Some shag devotees point to 1945 as the year beach music came to be. Others say that so-called beach music that year was just another point in the South's music continuum. Whatever happened, whenever it happened, proved remarkable. Blues, that songstress of the soul and chronicler of our desires, struggles, and imperfections, changed, and dancing would change with it.

Some say it rolled off the Mississippi, a mist that mesmerized all who breathed it. Others say it shot up from the river's alluvial plain, the Mississippi Delta. Something mystical, something melancholy came out of the delta all right—the blues, that sadly beautiful, beautifully sad music. And the blues, that mighty tributary of melody that grew out of work songs, spirituals, shouts, and chants, would shape shaggers' music. Aided and abetted by interplay with other cultural influences, the blues would forever change their lives.

"Beach cats" would throw away their socks, let their shoes fill with sand, and write a dance story southern to the core. But let's not get ahead of ourselves.

A MOMENTOUS RIVER

The story of the shag runs like a great river fed by tributaries aplenty. So many feeder streams merged to create the shag, it's impossible to identify them all. You might as well dip a cup of water from the Mississippi and try to identify its origin.

Many things had to fall into place for the shag to arise. The jukebox had to be invented. It and the 45-rpm would play a pivotal role in the shag culture by bridging the race divide. (Ironically the fabled jukebox got its name from the Gullah word "juke" or "joog," meaning rowdy or wicked.) Some shaggers could be rowdy, and some counted fisticuffs among their armaments when fueled by canned beer, which arrived in the mid-1930s.

The genesis for many cultural riches arrived on our shores from Africa, courtesy of one of humankind's darker ventures: the slave trade. Blacks who found themselves in the New World brought legacies, among them music and dancing.

Close your eyes and conjure up Ike Turner and his Kings of Rhythm belting out "Rocket 88" or even better Chuck Berry duck-walking with his Gibson guitar, ripping riffs while gliding along the stage. Few artists escaped the influence of this kind of showmanship, a gift from generations of blacks. And it was by no means the sole gift.

THE BLUES

One tributary runs strong and long: the blues. The African diaspora brought magic from villagers gathered around campfires beating rhythms on goatskin drums, playing flutes, and plucking stringed instruments. Their call-and-response songs featured improvisation, a backbeat, and syncopation—a pleasant disruption of the beat—that gave the music spellbinding rhythm. Within their songs lived the seeds for the blues.

Over the years the cadence carried over the sea, up creeks, across rice fields, over swamps, and into our souls. When he penned "Rock 'n Roll Music," Chuck Berry summed it up: "If it's got a backbeat, you can't lose it." Lost it was not. The blues flowed from the Mississippi Delta, a region that's given us more blues singers than all other southern states combined. Among the region's fabled bluesmen you'll find Bo Diddley, Howlin' Wolf, Muddy Waters, Willie Dixon, John Lee Hooker, and B. B. King. At the forefront was Robert Johnson, whom Eric Clapton deemed "the most important blues singer that ever lived." Legend says that Johnson made a deal with the devil at a crossroads, where the devil tuned Johnson's guitar and made him its master. Thus did the blues come to be.

There were lesser-known bluesmen, among them Tommy Johnson, Son House, and Charley Patton, and an influential but overlooked bluesman, Arthur Crudup ("That's All Right, Mama"). And that is but a start.

While sorrow and regret suffused blues singers' songs, lyrics often explored sexual motifs that would stitch many a shag melody together. Bluesmen's tales of love and loneliness would also surface in shag songs' timeless lyrics. Blues music wasn't set in concrete, though. The Chicago blues scene drifted away

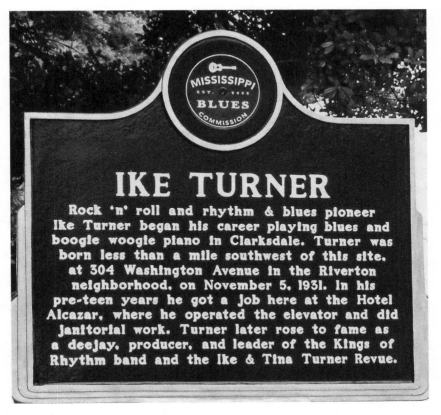

The Hotel Alcazar had a radio station. Ike Turner would run up to the second floor and look through the window at the guy spinning records. He invited Turner in and showed him how to hold a record. "Next thing I know, he was going across the street for coffee and leaving me in there alone. I was only eight. That was the beginning of my thing with music," said Turner.

Photograph by Brenda Haskins, courtesy Jim O'Neal,
BluEsoterica Archives & Mississippi Blues Trail.

from laments about life in Mississippi and spawned up-tempo blues popular in the 1940s known as "jump blues," a forerunner to rock 'n' roll.

"Race music" added Dark Continent currents to the river. Race records, 78-rpm gramophones made by and for African Americans in the 1920s and 1930s, preserved genres such as blues, jazz, and gospel music. Robert Johnson's 1936–37 recordings would reach into the future, helping bring the British Invasion thundering ashore in the 1960s.

Louis Jordan, "King of the Jukebox," soared to fame during the era of "radio segregation" when radio served as the lifeline for Americans, much as television and the Internet do today. It was a time when singers such as Bing Crosby and big-band leaders such as Sammy Kaye, Harry James, Glen Miller, and Les Brown and the Band of Renown dominated "white" charts. Many whites knew nothing of Jordan and his music. Jordan and his Tympani Five, however, ruled the 1940s "race" charts. His "Reconversion" placed high on the charts in 1945, and some consider it an early beach tune.

The music would change, and so would its nomenclature. Jerry Wexler of *Billboard* coined the term "rhythm and blues" in 1948 to replace the term "race music," which came from within the black community but seemed offensive in postwar America. In 1949 "Rhythm and Blues" replaced the *Billboard* category "Harlem Hit Parade."

Today the delta blues covers broad cultural terrain. It's so significant that the Mississippi Blues Commission had blues scholars and historians place interpretative markers—the Mississippi Blues Trail—to document the blues' development throughout Mississippi. Chicago has a marker, as it should. A marker with an asterisk should stand in Ocean Drive because that old "race music" would wield a major impact on beach music when people danced along the coast there.

THE MUSIC-RICH 1940S had begun with World War II raging. The Nazis invaded Denmark and Norway. The South Carolina coast saw its own invasion. A provocative, some said dangerous, dance overran the beach as the swing era faded.

World War II had brought hard times, and everyone had suffered. When General George S. Patton Jr. addressed his troops prior to Operation Overlord on June 5, 1944, he expressed the sentiments of many parents with sons and daughters in the war: "Sure, we want to go home. We want this war over with. The quickest way to get it over with is to go get the bastards who started it. The quicker they are whipped, the quicker we can go home."

Parents supporting war efforts had left their younger kids at home alone to perform household duties. Gas and butter rationing had driven home the point that times were tough. Sugar and coffee had been difficult to find. Nylon stockings with black seams up the back disappeared, so women without stockings painted black lines up the backs of their legs. Life went on. Besides, the hardships were nothing like the Great Depression, which brought out this line: "We were so poor, mama would bleach the coffee grounds and serve 'em as grits the next morning."

When Foreign Minister Shigemitsu and General Umezu of Japan signed the instruments of surrender aboard the USS *Missouri* on September 2, 1945, the country exhaled a mighty breath of relief. As the atomic ash settled, the United States emerged as the world's most powerful country. The war had mobilized the United States' capacity to produce goods, and Europe and other world markets laid low by war desperately needed U.S. products.

Postwar prosperity and a blossoming romance with the automobile ushered in the era of family vacations. The summer vacation would ascend to iconic status. One popular destination? A beach. And one popular beach rising above the rest? The Grand Strand. It was there and up the road a piece in North Carolina that the music would change and the dancing would change too.

The 1920s blues and 1930s country music had provided dark, rich loam for rock 'n' roll's roots. Gospel, folk, and blues in Memphis, Chicago, New Orleans, and other areas contributed to rock. A mishmash of music—swing, jazz, and more—had set people's feet to moving. Early rock 'n' roll featured a piano or saxophone as lead instrument, but the guitar—Robert Johnson's devilish instrument—would rise to prominence in the late 1950s.

A fellow by the name of Richard Penniman helped invent rock and roll. You know him as Little Richard. For the 1950s rock 'n' roll explosion, his "Tutti Frutti" served as the detonator. A-wop-bop-a-loo-lop, a-lop-bam-boo!

Shag music would evolve from the same purring river that produced rock. Artists such as Little Richard dropped colorful notes into the water that swirled, changed, and coalesced until brilliant new music emerged, though those rivers of rhythm remain a mysterious mélange.

In a similar vein, the shag's origins remain a bit of a riddle. North and South Carolinians have long debated the dance's origin, each claiming the shag as their own. In "The Myths, the Music & the Moves" (from *Livin' Out Loud* magazine, permission from Nancy Hall Publications), Teresa McLamb touches on the shag's imprecise origins: "Nothing stirs the pot in dance and music circles more than the question: Where and when was the shag invented?

Known as fas' dancing, the dirty shag, the Carolina shag, the bop, and other names, the phenomenon undoubtedly developed along the East Coast somewhere between Virginia Beach and Ocean Drive, but the legends of its evolution are varied and difficult to substantiate. Shag icon Harry Driver was once asked who the father of the shag was. His answer came back in just three words: 'I don't know.' What is certain is that its birth was in the exuberant spirit of teenagers excited by the soulful, sexy beat of rhythm and blues music."

Robert Plant's "Dancing in Heaven" might apply to the shag's exuberant spirit in the late 1940s and the 1950s. Shaggers felt like they had always been dancing in heaven, but the reality is they hadn't. A celebration in rhythm, yes, but it was not always this way. In the mid-1940s you couldn't find any black music in white clubs. There was no "beach music." Few people agree on the historical background that formed the shag, and trying to determine when the shag first became known by that name challenges researchers. One thing people agree on is the influence that Ocean Drive had on the dancers.

EVERY RIVER HAS ITS HEAD

The shag is a great river of dance, and Ocean Drive, South Carolina, forms its headwaters. It was where dancing along the coast would give birth to the term "beach music." It was also where shaggers would fall in love with the dance, times, and glory that would be theirs.

A vintage Tichnor Brothers postcard paints a picture of an Ocean Drive evening as pretty as, well, as pretty as a postcard. A full moon hangs over the Atlantic. Clouds catch moonbeams, suffusing the evening sky with soft luminescence. Windows spill yellow light. The name "Ocean Drive" graces a building and a movielike marquee, beyond which a couple embraces in the street.

As depicted in another postcard, an Ocean Drive evening in the late 1940s drew drivers of vintage Mercury coupes, Studebaker Commanders, and Desotos. People were inside. They had come to dance.

You'll find the roots of shag here where the cross-pollination of black music and white dancers took place. Dancing in O.D. would create memories that recall the smell of beer and salt air every time dancers would read, think, or hear about Ocean Drive and its fabled venues.

Ocean Drive—days here would take their place in legend, but not until a few intrepid dancers dared to cross the race line.

2

Crossing the Race Line

The music would just take you, like it does in church.

Lucretia Cayruth,
last original Big Apple dancer, the *State*

To understand how people fell in love with the shag, you have to understand the times that led to it and how they discovered the dance. You have to understand how life was for those who grew up in the first half of the last century. It was a time of taboos, a time when danger accompanied things we take for granted today.

It was a time when parents didn't approve of "race music" or the dancing and its settings. It was a time that called for bold moves and a willingness to do the unacceptable. Come, then, and see how things used to be, and see how things changed.

THE LIST READS like a roll call of superstars for a simple reason: it is. Envision a marquee ablaze with these names: Cab Calloway, Ray Charles, Duke Ellington, Ella Fitzgerald, Billie Holiday, Lena Horne, B. B. King, Wilson Pickett, Otis Redding, Little Richard, the Supremes, the Temptations, and Muddy Waters.

In the days of segregation, no bright lights heralded these legendary performers' presence. They may have played your town and no one, whites that is, knew it.

Their names blaze up in a place lost in time, a string of safe havens that provided black performers acceptable places to perform throughout the South and eastern states—the "Chitlin' Circuit." As for places to eat and sleep, well that was another matter thanks to a system—you could say, a racial caste system—with an odd but memorable name. Jim Crow laws controlled a way of life and practices that in effect maintained segregation in the South and bordering states from the late 1870s to the mid-1960s.

Viewed from the rearview mirror of the twenty-first century, Jim Crow laws and practices seem downright bizarre. In South Carolina in 1932, Jim Crow law decreed that all circuses and tent shows must provide separate entrances for whites and blacks. Another law deemed it unlawful for a Negro and a white person to play pool together.

These practices, first known as Black Codes, came to be known as "Jim Crow" laws, a strange term that invites interest. Lost in the dust of the old South, a man's name came to represent de jure segregation. Some historians believe that the term originated around 1830 when a white man with a blackened face, a minstrel performer named Thomas Dartmouth Rice, or "Daddy Rice," danced and pranced while singing the "Jump Jim Crow" song. Rice, as the story goes, had seen a crippled black man or boy down South dancing and singing a ditty:

> Come listen all you gals and boys I's jist from Tuckyhoe,
> I'm going to sing a little song, my name's Jim Crow,
> Weel about and turn about and do jis so,
> Eb'ry time I weel about and jump Jim Crow.

Whatever the origin, Jim Crow's role in the lyrics came to identify the segregation resulting from so-called separate-but-equal facilities that came about in a wrong-side-up way.

The Civil Rights Act of 1875 had sought to level the racial playing field: "All persons . . . shall be entitled to full and equal enjoyment of the accommodations, advantages, facilities, and privileges of inns, public conveyances on land or water, theaters, and other places of public amusement." The law, for the most part unenforceable, lasted but eight years.

In 1883 the Supreme Court ruled the Civil Rights Act of 1875 unconstitutional. Chief Justice Joseph Bradley maintained that the Fourteenth

Amendment offered blacks no protection from discrimination by private businesses and individuals, just protection from discrimination by states. Another court ruling in 1896, *Plessy v. Ferguson,* decreed that separate-but-equal facilities did not infringe on blacks' rights. A profusion of Jim Crow laws and practices sprang up.

A few such laws . . .

North Carolina . . . "The state librarian is directed to fit up and maintain a separate place for the use of the colored people who may come to the library for the purpose of reading books or periodicals."

South Carolina . . . "No persons, firms, or corporations, who or which furnish meals to passengers at station restaurants or station eating houses, in times limited by common carriers of said passengers, shall furnish said meals to white and colored passengers in the same room, or at the same table, or at the same counter."

"White Only" and "Colored" signs cleaved the races. South Carolina even banned swimming in state parks to keep the races separate. Blacks who wanted to see films in white theaters were often forced to sit in the balconies—ironic revenge to be visited on music-loving whites.

It was in this climate that Harper Lee's *To Kill a Mockingbird* was set in mid-1930s Alabama, 1936 to be precise. Lee's famed novel recounts the horrors that a black man, Tom Robinson, suffered after being falsely accused of raping a white girl.

Lee's novel, bejeweled with autobiographical facets, depicted southern life and racial injustice during the Jim Crow era, which was fraught with angst and second-guessing. If a black man offered to shake hands with a white man, it suggested social equality—a no-no. If a black man offered his hand to a white woman, rape accusations might come his way.

Hard to imagine whites and blacks on the same dance floor in such a climate, but not because white kids didn't want to dance among blacks. Remember Fat Sam's Big Apple Club in Columbia in 1936? The Big Apple dance craze began there, and it's a marker along one of the tributaries feeding the great shag river.

The Big Apple, and thus the shag, almost didn't come to pass. In *Beth Shalom, Keeping Columbia's Jewish Traditions Alive,* Cal Harrison reveals how Fat Sam's Big Apple Club might never had existed had a nine-hundred-dollar real-estate transaction been rescinded by a congregation worried that their hallowed old house of worship might fall into scandalous hands.

The real estate in question, the House of Peace, had replaced an earlier house of worship that burned in 1915. Around 1934 an expanding congregation was outpacing its capacity, and the congregation decided to build a new synagogue. The harsh financial times delayed the building of a new synagogue. Selling the old synagogue offered one way to raise funds. Six months later, however, no firm offers had been made.

Harrison wrote:

The building was finally sold in March 1936 to H. Desportes for $900. Because of "so much unfavorable criticism" of the sale, the board immediately voted to buy back the building, but the effort was dropped five months later when the board couldn't come to terms with the new owner.

The sale turned out to be scandalous to many members of the congregation. From 1936 to 1938, the old shul was converted into the Big Apple Night Club. The oak pews were removed but the stained-glass windows

THE BIG APPLE DOME

Today's domed ceiling reflects the original ceiling's heavenly bodies theme.
Photograph by Tom Poland.

remained. Neon lights in the shape of shooting stars and comets were added to the central dome and a giant red apple was painted on one of the walls.

Young blacks performed a circle dance as old as Africa, a group dance that came to be called the Big Apple. (Whoever painted that apple created an eponymous shrine.)

Harrison continued, "A delegation of Columbia dancers traveled to New York to demonstrate it, and much to the chagrin of House of Peace members, the Big Apple dance swept the nation in 1937, making the little nightclub famous."

Had H. Desportes resold the building back to the congregation, the Big Apple might never have happened. That would have eliminated the Little Apple. Where would the shag be today? But it happened, and the key to it all was music coming from an old synagogue.

BIG APPLE SEEDS

"On weekend nights in 1936, shouts would ring out from the old House of Prayer synagogue on Gates Street. Inside the Big Apple, as the club was known, young people would form a circle, steppin' out to the sweaty beat, waiting for their time to 'shine,'" Jeff Wilkinson wrote in the August 24, 2003, Sunday edition of the *State*. He continued:

> The steps were "called" like the square dance. The dancers would "swing left" or "swing right" in a circle until the "leaderman" called popular steps—"Spank Yo' Horsey," "Piggy Back" or "Scratchin' Fleas."
>
> The dancing was relentless and competitive—rug cuttin' with roots so deep it stretched all the way back to Africa. "It just came from inside of us," said Lucretia Cayruth.

The music must have been booming that auspicious night. As University of South Carolina students Donald Davis, Billy Spivey, and Harold "Goo-Goo" Wiles drove by Fat Sam's nightclub, music stopped them in their tracks. They got out of the car and asked the club's owner, Frank "Fat Sam" Boyd, for permission to enter. It was unusual for whites to go into a black club. Skip Davis, the son of Donald Davis, said, "Fat Sam made two conditions. They had to pay twenty-five cents each and they had to sit in the balcony."

The spellbound students watched blacks forming a big circle dancing. Watching, however, was all they could do. Feeling the sting of reverse segregation—after all, old Jim Crow was watching—they paid to sit in the balcony.

During the next few months, the white students brought more friends to watch the black dancers. "We had a lot of nickels with us because it took a nickel to play a song. If the music stopped and the people on the floor didn't have any money, we didn't get any more dancing. We had to feed the Nickelodeon," recalls Harold E. Ross.

Students would sit in the balcony studying and calling out dance steps. The dancers responded by jumping into the circle and "shining."

As Wilkinson wrote in the August 24, 2003, Sunday edition of the *State*, "In the following months at USC's fraternity and sorority houses, the dance would enter another phase. They looked forward to the end of school and the annual migration to the Grand Strand, anxious to 'polish the apple' at the Myrtle Beach Pavilion."

Harold Ross and others embraced the Big Apple's steps. "We always did the best we could to imitate the steps we saw," he said. "But we called it the

DANCERS AT FAT SAM'S
BIG APPLE CLUB

Steps as old as Africa are frozen in a shaglike pose. Wearing her partner's hat, she stares at the floor where a bit of the shag's genetic matter formed in 1936.

From the Augustus T. Graydon Collection.

THE BIG APPLE BALCONY

Tossing coins from this balcony, white students kept the nickelodeon playing
so they could watch the Big Apple dancers. The students called their version
the "Little Apple," a small-but-important step in the shag's evolution.

Photograph by Tom Poland.

Little Apple. We didn't feel like we should copy the Big Apple, so we called it
that."

Summer 1937—USC students dance the Big Apple at the pavilion in Myrtle
Beach. Word reached the New York talent agent Gay Foster, who auditioned
dancers in the Chatterbox, a club in the basement of Columbia's Jefferson
Hotel. He selected couples from South and North Carolina to go to the Roxy
Theatre for a three-week engagement starting September 3, 1937. After selling
out six performances a day, the Big Apple Dancers then hit the road for a six-
month cross-country tour, and the Big Apple craze arrived full force.

Life magazine featured the Big Apple in a four-page photo spread on
December 20, 1937, predicting that 1937 would be remembered as the year of
the Big Apple. It was, bringing more vexation to the House of Peace congregation. Ironically white dancers toured the country in 1937 and 1938 doing their

BIG APPLE STEPS

In 1936 USC students Donald Davis, Billy Spivey, and Harold "Goo-Goo"
Wiles walked down these steps carrying Little Apple seeds with them.

Photograph by Tom Poland.

rendition of a black dance. War approached, and the races remained apart
except for a few bold souls who crossed the line.

In *Shag, the Dance Legend,* Bo Bryan wrote, "During the war, the only people who heard a variety of rhythm and blues were a few hipsters here and there
who made a habit of jumping the Jim Crow rope." One such fellow was Mal-
colm Ray "Chicken" Hicks. Dancing was in his blood, as he learned to do the
Little Apple from girls up in Durham, North Carolina, when he was around
thirteen.

Hicks grew up around blacks, and it wasn't a big deal to watch blacks jitter-
bugging at a Durham armory. He slipped into many a "Colored Only" show.
Watching from the balcony—Jim Crow's reverse sting—Hicks saw new steps.
An innovator, he picked up dance moves wherever he saw them. Shag mythol-
ogy holds that Hicks picked up his distinctive dance step, the "camel walk,"
lounging around Skinny's Shoeshine Parlor in Durham.

BIG APPLE DOOR

In 1936 this door opened to reveal Big Apple dancers "polishing
the apple." It also opened a path to times when blacks and whites
could enjoy music and dance without Jim Crow's prying eyes.

Photograph by Tom Poland.

DANCE HISTORY WALKED THROUGH THESE DOORS

University of South Carolina students walked through these doors in 1936 to watch blacks dance wildly at Fat Sam's Big Apple Night Club in Columbia. The students took the dance to the Myrtle Beach Pavilion, and soon the Big Apple swept the nation.

Photograph by Tom Poland.

THE BASIC AT OD ARCADE

Face to face, an arm's length away, this couple performs "the basic," a fundamental step that helps dancers get the shag's rhythm and general movement. From here come other steps featuring movement and gracefulness.

Photograph by Robert Clark.

A BALANCED BLUR

With proper foot placements, shag movements
look fluid, balanced, and in rhythm.

Photograph by Robert Clark.

MEMORIES

Photographs are all that remain.
The Ocean Drive Pavilion is gone,
and so are its legends.

Photograph by Robert Clark.

NO MORE JIM CROW

With the days of Jim Crow's de facto segregation long gone, couples white and black hit the floor to dance to rhythm and blues' descendant, beach music.

Photograph by Robert Clark.

SHAGGERS' SIDEWALK OF FAME

Pavers commemorating legendary shaggers and granite markers representing shag clubs from the Eastern Seaboard pave Main Street in Ocean Drive, South Carolina.

Photograph by Robert Clark.

MOVEMENT AND GRACE

Shaggers aren't supposed to watch their feet; yet many do.
The emphasis on footwork rather than turns lowers many
an eye toward the floor, but that doesn't ruin the beauty.

Photograph by Robert Clark.

DREAMING WITH THEIR FEET

A shagger's ghostly step trails across a worn floor. Plywood, sand, cement—the surface doesn't matter to shaggers. All that matters are the music, the partner, and the dance.

Photograph by Robert Clark.

BOOGIE WOOGIE BOYS

Atlantic Groove's two-piece brass section blows it out at Fat Harold's Beach Club. Among their popular music genres you'll find Carolina Beach. Many white bands took up the black sound.

Photograph by Robert Clark.

BIG APPLE DANCE FLOOR

No jukebox, no dancers, no nickels raining from the balcony. The Historic
Columbia Foundation purchased the Big Apple in 1993, and it now hosts
weddings, parties, luncheons, and special events. Time dances on.

Photograph by Tom Poland.

As Bryan tells it, Hicks became acquainted with some black men who took
him to joints in a Durham township known as Haiti. There he came to love
blues, jazz, and gospel. When the big bands hit Durham, Hicks was in the
balcony "watching for a chance to slip downstairs and boogie with the black
girls," according to Bryan.

In "Who Is Chicken Hicks," Benn Steelman of Wilmington's *StarNews*
wrote of Hicks's colorful past and his last exploits as a shagger:

Well known on the Eastern Seaboard from Virginia to Florida, Hicks
regularly performed exhibitions at the Grand National dance championships in Atlanta; his last appearance there was on Memorial Day weekend
2004, just weeks before his death. He was admitted to the Shaggers Hall
of Fame, and the Cape Fear Museum displays his signature white "shaggin" shoes.

BIG APPLE MARKER

Photograph by Tom Poland.

Hicks served in the U.S. Coast Guard, then, by his own account washed up in Carolina Beach in 1943. Back then he said, "It was like a state fair, 24 hours a day. . . . There were places that had no doors, 'cause they were always open."

DANCING ON THE NORTH CAROLINA COAST

Hicks, his younger brother Bobby, and their pals would drive to a beautiful, historic coastline where pirates once roamed, lighthouses became legends, a colony vanished, and man learned to fly. It would also be a coastline where kids dared to discover wonderful music.

Back then you couldn't just flip a switch and find black music. Radio and the recording industry had yet to undergo the cultural revolution of the 1950s that would bring African American music and performers to the forefront.

Brendan Greaves and Michael C. Taylor conducted extensive ground-level studies on the shag, and Hicks's penchant for finding black music plays a prominent role in their work. Greaves and Taylor's chapbook on the shag originated from their graduate fieldwork in folklore at the University of North Carolina in Chapel Hill. Their work points out the difficulty in nailing down the shag's history, an often-heard refrain. They give Hicks an amount of credit for pioneering the shag similar to what Billy Jeffers received: "Despite the fact that the myriad musical and social strands that ultimately coincided to give rise to the beach and shag music phenomena are hydra-headed, murky, and ambiguous, the oft-told legend holds that beach music was born at Jim Hanna's Tijuana Inn at Carolina Beach, North Carolina, in the spring of 1948. It was here that Hanna, a former merchant marine, first placed African American jump blues on his piccolo, or jukebox, at the behest of his friend Chicken Hicks, creating a space where white listeners and dancers could engage the largely taboo black music in a space easily entered and exited, both literally and figuratively."

In the June 13, 2006, online issue of *YES! Weekly*, Ogi Overman wrote that Hanna

called the amusement company in Wilmington that stocked the jukebox in his establishment and had them bring over some of that music they regularly took to the joints down the road.

Soon the box that sat just to the right of the entrance to the long and narrow club was blaring tunes unheard of in postwar white America. . . . Suddenly white America and black America had learned to coexist, if only at the jukebox at the Tijuana Inn.

Shag emissary Hicks and his memorable looks had made a remarkable contribution to music. Bryan's *Shag* described Hicks as "tall and rail-thin with arms as long as railroad ties, skinny as toothpicks with sledgehammers attached at the business ends." At Carolina Beach it didn't take long for Hicks's inclination to visit black clubs to take hold. Hicks and the boys would hit the dance scene in black "jump joints."

Greaves and Taylor wrote: "According to legend, Hicks was a Durham-raised ruffian with an affinity for black music and white liquor. On his nigh weekly moonshine-purchasing trips from Carolina Beach to the neighboring African American community of Seabreeze, Hicks regularly heard contemporary popular songs by black artists such as Joe Liggins and The Honeydrippers, Louis Jordan and His Tympani Five, Lionel Hampton, and Wynonie Harris, all progenitors of the nascent jump-blues style that was emerging out of the swing and big band traditions."

Hicks began to show off some of the new bop and jitterbug steps he'd picked up from Seabreeze. "I'm gone tell you the truth, I didn't call it anything," he said in 1996. "I couldn't stand it, how they all called it the jitterbug. All I said was, 'Come on, let's go jump awhile.'" His favorite white jump joint, he later recalled, was the Sugar Bowl, at the south end of Carolina Beach.

Hicks's propensity for visiting black nightclubs again paid dividends: he heard new music and learned new moves. When he hit the dance floor, people gathered around for the show. Hicks, however, was more than an exceptional dancer. He was also an agent of change. He changed the music whites listened to. He helped bring blacks' "bop" sound to whites, and that, in part, would lead to the rise of the "beach music" sound.

As Greaves and Taylor wrote, "After no small amount of prodding, he convinced Hanna to have the jukebox servicing company install some of this music on the Tijuana Inn's piccolo." ("Piccolo" is Harlem slang for "jukebox.")

"I got chummy with the jukebox changers," Hicks said in a 1996 interview, "and I'd say 'Bring that record and that record.' I got rid of Glenn Miller in Carolina Beach jukeboxes."

Change was swift, as Greaves and Taylor noted. "You couldn't get in the place," said Hanna. "People just loved the music."

The music proved infectious, and people adored its source: the jukebox. As the nation was coming out of the Great Depression, the jukebox secured a reverent place in Americana and shagdom. In a time when few people could afford their own phonographs, a nickel provided a way to hear great music. A designer's dream, the jukebox's colors, bubbles, and swirls transported people to another world, and it gave black music exposure. It enriched the shaggers' musical tastes and heritage and spread the shag up and down the North and South Carolina coast.

According to Steelman: "By 1948, shagging had broken out at Carolina Beach's Ocean Plaza. The following year, however—after a spate of fistfights between local boys and servicemen (and a couple of rumored killings)—the mayor of Carolina Beach ordered a crackdown. The Tijuana Inn and Sugar Bowl were closed, along with a couple of other places . . . Hicks may have had to leave town for a while. (He never left for long.) The only dance hall left, the Ocean Plaza, limited dancers to ages 18 and older, so by 1950, the shag scene shifted down the coast to Myrtle Beach."

DROP ANOTHER NICKEL IN

Song-popularity counters told jukebox owners how many times each record played.
The result? Popular records remained, while songs played less often were replaced.

Photograph by Robert Clark.

Harry Driver remembered the fighting that shifted shag history in a big way. "The dance floor was always crowded with servicemen on those Saturday nights and their tempers matched the hard-driving tempos of the music," said Driver. "The fights were so numerous that two policemen and two MPs were always around to keep the club from turning into a war zone. After spending some time in these jump joints as they were called, you learned to duck, do some fancy footwork, and most importantly, how to spot the troublemakers and totally avoid them."

The fights, according to Driver, were furious and fast: "When the fights started, they were quick, brutal, and always bloody. The intent was not to win a short bout but to inflict permanent damage." Bottles, added Driver, were favorite weapons.

MUSIC BUILT A BRIDGE

Soon other jump joints opened along Carolina Beach. Simply shacks, each provided the basics: a dance floor, a jukebox, and black music. More and more

CHICKEN HICKS AND HARRY DRIVER, 1994

Fabled beach cats Hicks, left, and Driver duel it out, sans fisticuffs. Some consider Driver the "father of the shag." Hicks (here without his signature white shoes) danced to fame all along the Eastern Seaboard. The Cape Fear Museum displays Hicks' signature white "shaggin'" shoes.

Photograph courtesy of Ellen Taylor.

young people could now dance to off-limits black music. The blues began to boil in places beyond the beach.

Katherine Cagle grew up in the mountains of southwest Virginia and remembers how the music's true roots helped bring the races together: "My white friends and I listened to rhythm and blues on WLAC radio, Nashville, and on Sunday nights we loved the black gospel music that sounded much like the rhythm and blues. We loved Chuck Berry and Fats Domino and Little Richard."

The white kids loved Little Richard, and no Jim Crow balcony could hold them. In "Antics in Candyland," Candice Dyer quoted Little Richard from *The Life and Times of Little Richard: The Quasar of Rock,* an authorized biography by BBC's "Dr. Rock," Charles White: "We played places where they told us not to come back because the kids got so wild. They were tearing up the streets and throwing bottles and jumping off the theater balconies at shows. At that time, the white kids had to be up in the balcony—they were 'white spectators.' But then they'd leap over the balcony to get downstairs where the black kids were."

Black music was catching on, as Greaves and Taylor described:

Following Hanna's loading of the Tijuana Inn's piccolo with African American music, other entrepreneurs opened their own "jump joints" up and down the Carolina Beach strand within weeks. These venues were barebones affairs, often consisting of a tin roof, a dance floor, and, most importantly, a jukebox that, for a nickel, would play the popular African-American music of the day. These jukeboxes were frequently chained to the floor to prevent patrons from stealing the money or, more significantly, the records. While Hanna's Tijuana Inn first provided drinking-age crowds access to black jump blues, these anonymous beach establishments provided underage kids a way to participate with the African-American music and dance that was at once taboo and coveted.

The income from the newly thriving Tijuana Inn, in combination with his enterprising nature, provided Hanna with the resources to convert a former bowling alley across the street from the Tijuana Inn into a dance hall, which he christened Bop City. The new establishment served as ground zero for further Caucasian exploration of African-American artists such as Paul Williams and Sticks McGhee, white artists playing black music such as Jimmy Cavallo and The Houserockers, and the burgeoning dance movement called the shag.

But how did that burgeoning dance movement get its name? Theories abound, among them one served up by Johnie Davis, who lives in Carolina Beach, North Carolina. He's president of the Cape Fear Shag Club and a charter member of the O.D. Social Pavilion and Shag Club in Ocean Drive. As quoted in *Livin' Out Loud* magazine (with permission from Nancy Hall Publications), Davis said that his aunt Gladys McAdams was "the jitterbug queen of Carolina Beach" and that she taught Chicken Hicks to dance.

Davis provided one possible origin of the term "shag." He said:

In the late 1930s and early 1940s during World War II, there was a little village just across the bridge from Carolina Beach called Seabreeze. This was a beach destination for African Americans as they could not visit "white only" beaches. In Seabreeze there were many juke joints, chicken shacks, and boarding houses and hotels that catered to blacks from all over. The dancing there was "boogie-woogie" to very old rhythm and blues music like the Spaniels, Orioles, and Ink Spots, among others.

During that time, GIs were returning home from tours in Europe and had heard the word "shag" over there in an entirely different meaning. Some of those young white boys would slip through the woods at night and watch the dancing. Legend says that someone said, "It looks like they are shagging." Those boys would come back over the bridge and visit the joints in Carolina Beach and try to copy those dancers and add their own twist to it.

According to Davis, the dance continued to be called fast dancing for quite a while. "It wasn't called shagging because that was thought to be naughty," he said. For a while people called the dance the "dirty shag." Nevertheless locals began to copy or emulate the dancing they saw, "and that's how shagging came about." Davis, while acknowledging the many stories about Ocean Drive, is certain that the dance started at Carolina Beach in 1946. He remembers the old haunts, the Tijuana Inn, the Rec Hall, the Ocean Plaza Hotel (the OP), a pavilion, and small places with just a jukebox each—simple affairs as Greaves and Taylor describe. Wrightsville Beach, Davis added, had the Lumina Pavilion and other smaller places.

Earlier the dancing underwent change inland as well. The May 28, 2000, *Fayetteville Observer* reported that the "Shag Queen" Clarice Reavis was dancing in the 1930s at White Lake's Goldston Beach, where the White Lake Pavilion jutted over the water. She danced at USO clubs in Fayetteville too. "I was dancing myself to death," said Reavis. "We were doing the rock 'n' roll as hard as we could. . . . And then we started to slow it down after a while."

So where did the two races converge on the dance floor? The answer remains out of focus, a blend of black and white, gray for sure.

Little Richard aside, Bryan gets us close. He wrote in *Shag* that white kids would leave their beach houses in O.D. to go to Myrtle Beach. They were, without doubt, sneaking over to a black nightclub in Whispering Pines. They were, as Bryan wrote, "jumping the Jim Crow rope" to watch black jitterbugs at big-band extravaganzas, some of which reputedly featured Count Basie.

The place with so much allure for white kids? It was a way station along the Chitlin' Circuit, but not just any way station.

3

Music Builds a Bridge

*I may be helping to bring harmony
between people through my music.*

Nat King Cole

Once upon a time a place called Whispering Pines stood on Carver Street in Myrtle Beach. A gem of a black club once operated at Whispering Pines: Charlie's Place.

Frank Beacham, a New York City journalist from Honea Path, South Carolina, wrote "This Magic Moment, When the Ku Klux Klan Tried to Kill Rhythm and Blues Music in South Carolina," an excerpt of which appears in *Toward the Meeting of the Waters*. The story of Charlie's Place appears in Beacham's book *Whitewash: A Journey through Music, Mayhem and Murder.* "Charlie's Place, Shaggin' the Night Away" is Beacham's third version of a story from Charlie Fitzgerald, a chic black New York entrepreneur who ran a way station at the intersection of the shag and the Chitlin' Circuit.

Black performers came to entertain on the Chitlin' Circuit, a string of clubs and joints throughout the South where singers and musicians could do their thing in a safe, acceptable venue. Finding a place to eat and a room for the night was another matter. Entertainers destined for greatness had to rely on accommodations with friends. That's the way it was in the era of Jim

Crow—that time for blacks of sitting in the back of the bus, of drinking from water coolers marked "Colored Only." Nor, in a bit of reverse discrimination, could whites mix with blacks to enjoy music, but some did.

The pines began whispering, as Beacham wrote, the night Billie Holiday sang there. Thus came the name Whispering Pines. Other black performers destined for greatness came to Charlie's Place, including Little Richard.

Fitzgerald ran his club without foolishness, and Charlie's Place earned a reputation as a peaceful establishment. That didn't head off trouble. As Beacham wrote, "Fitzgerald's coziness with whites was out of sync with the time and place. Racial tension in South Carolina began escalating after a federal judge opened the state's Democratic primary to black voters in 1948. It was to the chagrin of many Southern whites that blacks began to assume a few positions of power."

The times and tensions conspired to make Charlie a marked man. He stood out as wealthy and fearless. He did as white people did, including going into a restaurant and sitting down. Another sin bedeviled him: letting white kids into his place to hear the marvelous black entertainers.

Milford Powell was one such kid. He remembers going to Charlie's Place in 1952 to watch the dancing. "It wasn't called the shag," said Powell. "Back then, most folks from North Carolina called the shag the 'fas' dance."

Fast dance they did, particularly to a song Powell remembers hearing often at Charlie's Place, Lloyd Price's "Lawdy Miss Clawdy." This eight-bar blues tune with a rollicking piano backup became the biggest rhythm and blues hit of the year. It sold more than one million copies by crossing over to the white market. "The dancers went crazy to that song," said Milford, who added, "we danced for fun. It wasn't about how many steps you knew. It was about smoothness."

Fun, "race" music, dancing, and whites and blacks under the same roof made a taboo blend in those Jim Crow days. That the KKK would pay Charlie a visit was inevitable.

On August 26, 1950, the nightriders drove by Charlie's Place. Beacham remembers:

In an intimidating visit to his club, Klan members demanded that white patrons no longer be admitted. "They told Charlie they didn't want the white kids there listening to music," said Hemingway (Henry "Pork Chop" Hemingway, Myrtle Beach's first black policeman and Charlie's friend). "Charlie told them to go to hell. They warned him they were coming back."

At 9 P.M. on Saturday, August 26, 1950, the Klan staged a motorcade through the streets of Myrtle Beach. Scores of nightriders, outfitted in white KKK regalia, cruised the town in dozens of automobiles. The lead car had a fiery cross made up of glowing red electric light bulbs mounted on its left fender. . . . The Klan motorcade snaked slowly through the black neighborhoods of Myrtle Beach. Eventually it reached Carver Street, the automobile-lined roadway used by club-goers for parking during visits to Charlie's Place. As the intimidating convoy passed his crowded establishment, Fitzgerald became enraged. He picked up the phone and called the Myrtle Beach Police Department, warning that if the Klan returned, there would be bloodshed.

Instead of providing the club with protection, police passed Fitzgerald's message directly to Klan members, who took it as a dare. "Ladies and gentlemen, we being white Americans could not ignore that dare from a Negro," Hamilton, an organizer of the parade, recalled later at a Klan gathering.

Just before midnight, about sixty klansmen [*sic*] in twenty-five vehicles —this time with sirens silenced—made a return trip to Charlie's Place. Fifty-nine-year-old Charlie Fitzgerald waited defiantly for the white-sheeted mob outside the club. He was six feet, three inches tall, 190 pounds, balding, with a thin mustache. In each hand he gripped a pearl-handled pistol.

The arrival of the nightriders was swift and violent. A furious rush of ghost-like men streamed from the cars, immediately striking Fitzgerald in the face and seizing his weapons. Overwhelmed, he was tied up with a rope and thrown into the trunk of a klansman's car. There, locked in darkness, he listened helplessly as windows were smashed, tables and chairs overturned, and a volley of more than five hundred rounds of ammunition was sprayed into the wooden building that held his friends and customers.

"People were screaming, hollering, running everywhere. And the police were nowhere to be seen," said Leroy Brunson, who witnessed the attack as an eight-year-old boy. Suddenly, in the midst of the fury, the music stopped. The club's jukebox—the most powerful symbol of the cultural fusion that had united young blacks and whites in the postwar years— skipped, sputtered, and went silent as it was riddled by a hail of bullets. . . . After wrecking the club, the Klan members—with Charlie Fitzgerald still locked in the trunk of a car—quickly left the scene.

Fitzgerald survived, but things were never the same. Some whites were afraid to return to Charlie's Place. Many blacks left the area, and some said Charlie turned a bit mean. He had reason to; he was arrested many many times on trumped-up charges.

The nightriders' raid on Charlie's Place upset white and black residents. Beacham said: "After publicly denouncing the violence at the nightclub, Myrtle Beach Mayor J. N. Ramsey offered a tepid explanation for what triggered the attack. 'Some of the conditions that probably caused the Klan to parade through this particular area of Myrtle Beach, namely white people patronizing colored business establishments or visiting in colored sections for amusement purposes, are not approved by the Southern people generally, but they are absolutely legal,' the mayor said in a written statement after the shooting."

Five days later in a live radio address carried by Myrtle Beach and Conway radio stations, Sheriff Sasser cleared Fitzgerald of any crime related to the attack and said he had found no evidence that any Negro had fired a gun in the fracas.

Beacham later reported: "The sheriff denied a widespread rumor that Charlie's Place had been attacked because Fitzgerald 'was keeping a white woman for immoral purposes.' He did suggest, however, that the young white dancers who frequented the nightclub had influenced the Klan's actions. 'To my knowledge, some white men and women do go to this place on special occasions to hear the orchestra and watch the colored people dance,' the sheriff said. 'I have on many occasions told them it was not a good policy.'"

Not a good policy: that sums up the stance much of white society took during the era of Jim Crow. Back then "White Only" signs were posted everywhere. No signs were posted saying "No Dancing to Race Music," however, and dancing to race music happened.

Charlie's Place played a significant role in the coalescing of black music, white dancers, and black musicians. Beacham reported: "Though Charlie Fitzgerald's contributions are unknown to the thousands of white shaggers who keep the dance alive more than a half century later, the influence of his club—and the crossover of black music to a white audience—are repeatedly cited by the pioneers credited with inventing South Carolina's state dance."

"Black music influenced us from the start, and the only good place to hear it was on the Hill," said Billy Jeffers, who died in 2005. A popular jitterbugger and Shaggers Hall of Fame member, Jeffers began working at the Carolina beaches in the summer of 1938. He said, "We learned to smooth it out and do more with just a little bit of music. Being there made you think you were at the best place in the world."

Clarice Reavis, drawn to black music, went to the Hill, as did Harry Driver. According to Driver, "Leon Williams credits blacks at Charlie's Place and other clubs with helping white dancers feel the music. 'Colored people felt the music and that's why they can dance. When they feel the music, you can't teach them to count 1, 2, 3, 4. If they feel like wiggling when they feel the music, that's what is called "dirty." But it was never our intent to create a dirty dance. And it wasn't the colored people's intent either. They did the same thing in church. You might think they are getting with it, but they are just feeling the music.'"

Harry Driver, considered the "Father of the Shag" by some, lived in Dunn, North Carolina, all his life. He started going to Ocean Drive when he was around twelve. He recalled listening to "race" and Hit Parade music in 1945 at White Lake's Crystal Club during World War II, when German submarines prowled coastal waters and blackouts forced the dancers inland. There they danced to "suggestive" music banned in the segregated Carolinas. The bans mattered not.

Of the race music dancing, Driver said, "We had integration twenty-five years before Martin Luther King [Jr.] came on the scene. We were totally integrated because the blacks and whites had nothing in our minds that made us think we were different. We loved music, we loved dancing, and that was the common bond between us."

Not far from Dunn at the Williams Lake Pavilion in Sampson County, North Carolina, folks danced to the likes of the Tams, Martha Reeves and the Vandellas, Jackie Wilson, the Platters, and the Zodiacs.

Music was building a bridge between the races. It opened doors to yet-to-be-discovered musicians. As an amalgam of music interest swirled and eddied in backwoods and dark corners, musicians destined for greatness were taking baby steps toward fame, steps that, along with dance moves, moved the races toward convergence. White rockabilly and black gospel artists shared notes, licks, and wails as a new kind of music took form.

Struggling artists made something special from nothing. Case in point: hardscrabble musician Carl Perkins. Perkins grew up the son of poor sharecroppers near Tiptonville, Tennessee. Gospel music caught his ear at a young age, as was the case for many southerners. Walking into the white glare of cotton fields as a mere six-year-old picker, he loved black field workers' music. And Saturday nights brought dreams into his home via a wonder called radio —the Grand Ole Opry.

Roy Acuff caught Perkins's ear, and the kid asked his parents for a guitar. He might as well have asked for a pink Cadillac. Carl's dad made a rudimentary guitar from a cigar box and a broomstick. Later, Perkins's father spent a few bucks for a beat-up Gene Autry signature model guitar with worn-out strings.

Perkins tried what he heard from the Opry on his guitar. In the cotton fields John Westbrook took Perkins under his wing. "Uncle John," a sixty-something African American, played blues and gospel on a rickety acoustic guitar. He gave Perkins advice on how to play a guitar: "Get down close to it. You can feel it travel down the strangs, come through your head, and down to your soul where you live. You can feel it. Let it vib-a-rate."

GO, CAT, GO

Music skills come in strange ways. Perkins's guitar strings constantly broke. They proved no barrier to Perkins. Painful, yes, but a barrier, no. Just the opposite. With no money for new strings, he tied them together. Because the knots cut his fingers when sliding to another note, Perkins "bent" the notes, creating by chance a "blue note" played at a lower pitch than normal. A technique that grew out of necessity gave Perkins his sound, and he was on his way.

Perkins's story is by no means an oddity. Other stories like his exist in the merging of the races and music and dance. Trying to unravel the black-white path to rock and what would become shag music isn't easy. In fact it seems contradictory, but it is not. Dig deep enough, and you'll connect the dots.

In the 1960s British rockers adored the delta blues and idolized Elvis and Perkins. Free of racial restrictions, they repackaged and imported American black music to us. We called it rock 'n' roll, and it had kissing cousins we already knew. Beach music would come from the music Brits loved so much; thanks to Jim Crow, we just didn't recognize its roots.

Blues singers from South and North Carolina, of all places—not Mississippi, mind you—gave a British rock band destined for fame and glory its name. One story goes that Syd Barrett, a founding member, had a record by Pink Anderson of Laurens, South Carolina, and a record by Floyd Council, a bluesman born in Chapel Hill, North Carolina.

Another story goes that Barrett noticed the bluesmen's names in the liner notes of a 1962 Blind Boy Fuller album. However Barrett came across the bluesmen, he juxtaposed the first names of Pink Anderson and Floyd Council to get Pink Floyd, a monster of psychedelic and progressive rock. One album they'd produce, "Dark Side of the Moon," would dominate the charts as no album has. It is, most probably, the greatest rock album ever recorded. How ironic that this group named after South and North Carolina bluesmen would do its part to sustain the "dark ages" (the shag's years of retreat) staying on the charts an astounding 741 weeks from 1973 to 1988, longer than any album in history.

Blues repackaged and sent to us across the Atlantic as rock would change the music and dance scene. It all began when we were occupied with keeping the races apart and yet listening to Motown. Beach music too grew out of the blues.

In *The Rockin' 50s: The Decade That Transformed the Pop Music Scene* is an interview by Arnold Shaw with the pop music emissary Jerry Wexler. Wexler said:

> During my first year (with Atlantic Records, 1953), I cut Ruth Brown, the Clovers, Joe Turner, and the Drifters with Clyde. In those years, a top R&B record could go to four hundred thousand. Sales were localized in ghetto markets. There was no white sale and no white radio play. . . .
>
> At some point, we became aware that Southern whites were buying our records. . . . In May or June we always came out with what was known as a "beach record." It would be a hit in the pavilions—the bathing places—all through the Carolinas. We never missed.

Wexler knew that popular deejays could stampede youths into buying records. In the segregated South, however, deejays didn't play race music; but jukeboxes could. Wexler loved R&B. Did Atlantic Records take its name from Atlantic Beach, South Carolina, known as the "Black Pearl," one of African Americans' most popular resorts during segregation? Did Wexler, that sly fox, find a way to help Hicks and a fellow named "Big George" Lineberry load race records on white jukeboxes? We'll never know. Wexler died on August 15, 2008.

"'Sh-Boom' and the Bomb: A Postwar Call and Response" appeared in the *Columbia Journal of American Studies* in 2006. In it James M. Salem, professor emeritus of American Studies at the University of Alabama, discussed the jukebox's influence, among other things, following World War II: "The jukebox turned out to be a wonderfully efficient mechanism for the diffusion of black music, since an estimated 40 percent of all phonograph records at the time were sold to juke box operators. Jim Parker, a major R&B collector, jukebox historian, and participant in the Southern beach scene, remembers dancing to Atlantic records on the juke box [*sic*] with as many as six hundred white youth at a single pavilion. But high school and college kids who visited the beach pavilions returned home to Charleston, Charlotte, Atlanta, or Tuscaloosa and discovered where they could buy the records they had danced to. This created a crisis for the guardians of Southern racial purity."

Later Salem discussed the song that bridged two music cultures: "'Sh-Boom,' written and performed by five men no one had ever heard of (the Chords), in a genre that penetrated less than 6 percent of the music business (Rhythm & Blues), recorded by a small, independent label dedicated to producing black music in black styles by black performers for black customers (Atlantic Records), was released on an Atlantic subsidiary label that failed and died after twenty records (Cat records). Nevertheless, inspired by the sound of a nuclear explosion, 'Sh-Boom' is often credited as being the transitional song between R&B and rock 'n' roll, which is to say it was the song that turned a marginal music restricted to a minority sub-culture into a mainstream music that fascinated American youth first and world youth next."

IN THE LATE 1940S a few radio stations played rhythm and blues, and people heard the songs inland around lakes and rivers at small joints. Dances at teen canteens and National Guard armories also exposed people to what some would call "beach music."

Rigid barriers would soften as the big-band era died. The color line began to wash out, bleached by black musicians' crossover to white audiences, aided and abetted by guys like Hicks who got their records into white jukeboxes. Vinyl from artists such as Bull Moose Jackson and LaVern Baker could now be heard.

"You could only hear that stuff when you were at the beach and away from your parents," said one veteran shagger. "The whites loved what they heard and no sheriff was going to hold them back."

As black musicians and whites mixed, distinctions separating white and black cultures began to dissolve. The tight control of black music began to loosen as independent record labels and independent radio stations offered white kids black dance music.

Whereas big-band swing music dazzled listeners with its incredible trumpet and sax players, blacks' rhythm and blues soul set feet to moving. Groups such as the Drifters, Dominoes, and Temptations slowed the beat to better accommodate vocal arrangements. Thanks to Wexler, Atlantic Records, Hicks, and others, the real deal was close by. In 1947 black music was playing near Carolina Beach, North Carolina.

Kids, college students, and beach bums loved what they heard. As Jim Hanna had proclaimed, they loved this music with deep roots in the delta blues. The ghost of Robert Johnson was "on the beach." Dancers began to slow their tempo; they began to put more emphasis on the music's beat; they began to keep their feet on the ground, rejecting the jitterbug's wild antics and acrobatics. A measure of necessity underlay the slower tempo. The old shag haunts had no air-conditioning other than sea breezes. An unhurried pace allowing intricate moves beat the heat while allowing dance breakthroughs.

The shag differed from the jitterbug with its 360-degree spin, the pivot, and subtle nuances. Dancers, parting ways with the jitterbug, chose to go the way of glossy, silky moves, keeping their feet close to the ground. A small, packed dance floor didn't have room for flailing arms. Besides, the idea was to be cool. Dancers with aspirations picked up moves from more accomplished dancers fantasizing how other dancers would clear the floor for them. As one shagger put it, "They began to dream with their feet."

Bryan's *Shag, the Dance Legend* states that a kid from Florence, South Carolina, Billy Jeffers, was among the first to slow the tempo of the "fast dancers." Often credited with begetting the shag, Jeffers, a velvety jitterbugger par excellence, made a comment that revealed shag's emerging code: "When a dancer lifted his feet above a certain height he was asked to either leave or sit down."

Despite Jeffers's accolades, no one dancer gets credit for the shag. A demure Jeffers discounted any notion that he was the father of the shag. The innovations of many morphed into this smooth, sophisticated dance movement.

What of this new dance? Remember the Twist? Remember the Macarena? Where is the Charleston? Where is the Big Apple? The shag and its deep cultural roots proved far more enduring. Shabby ambassadors, bums turned master shaggers spread it to other beaches. Mesmerized onlookers took up the cause, and shagging at the pavilions put a lasting imprint on shag's first wave of lovers. They fell in love with a shrine known simply as O.D.

4

Legendary Days at Ocean Drive

After too many years of doing without, thanks to the Depression and World War II shortages, families thronged to Atlantic beaches in the late 1940s and early 1950s. From Virginia Beach down through Carolina Beach to Charleston and Savannah, beaches made tempting vacation destinations for families, their shiny new cars, and their cash. In South Carolina rustic venues for summer escape shot up from coastal sand. Cherry Grove, Ocean Drive, Crescent Beach, Atlantic Beach, Surfside, and Garden City joined Myrtle Beach and Pawley's Island as summer havens.

Teens in vacationing families idled away afternoons swimming and slathering iodine and baby oil over their bodies. Come sundown, they headed for the pavilions. Bingo, pinball machines, skee ball, and other arcade games amused the kids. They could also dance—the pavilions had jukeboxes and dance floors—something far more addictive than arcade games.

Upon returning home, jubilant kids spread the news about the beach nightlife and the pavilions. A case of summer euphoria gripped them, and a social shift of sorts began. Teens with incurable cases of beach fever returned to the beach summer after summer to land jobs as lifeguards, bingo callers, waitresses, and bowling alley pinsetters. They took jobs of all sorts if those enabled them to spend another summer at the beach.

Their lives had a simple rhythm: working by day and dancing by night. Ocean Drive produced its share of great dancers: Burt Bennett, Jimmy Calcutt, Lacy Moore, Vera Munn, Bubber Snow, Leon Williams, and others. Life was simple, and life was good. You could drive onto the beach, and a quarter bought a hotdog; another quarter bought a beer—that's right, a beer. A nickel bought one song on a jukebox; a quarter bought six tunes. Fellows who leaned on the jukebox had a shot at meeting girls dropping coins into the colorful melody maker.

Partying and dancing, with a good measure of romance thrown in, made for a great summer. It was said that more virgins came to the beach than went back home. The word about the girls got around, luring young men to the beach anyway possible. Fifteen-year-old photographer-to-be Jack Thompson hitchhiked to Myrtle Beach in 1951 with pals Carroll A. Campbell, a future governor and Shaggers Hall of Famer, and Fred Collins, a future amusement industry baron. Jack related those formative days to the Horry County Oral History Project: "Those were wonderful times here when the dancing craze started in the late '40s. . . . The pavilion would be packed with people around the old jukebox." Around 1953 or 1954, he said, some cool cats from North

OCEAN DRIVE WATER TANK

The Society of Stranders logo adorns the North Myrtle Beach water tank. Designed by S.O.S. artist in residence Becky Stowe, the tank's message is clear: you're in shag country.

Photograph by Robert Clark.

SONNY'S PAVILION

Sonny Nixon first put up a gazebo with a jukebox in 1947. In 1949 he built his famed pavilion. When Hurricane Hazel passed through October 15, 1954, it left nothing of Sonny's Pavilion. For many old school shaggers, things were never the same. This sign hangs at the Ocean Drive Arcade today.

Photograph by Robert Clark.

Carolina and Carolina Beach slowed the tempo: "Instead of jumping up and down, they wanted to move side to side and swing their hips."

City fathers sent the police to arrest the hip shakers for indecent exposure. "Night after night," said Thompson, "the popular dancers were dragged off the dance floor by the nape of the neck and seat of the pants and were hauled off to jail." Kids worked the crowd with milkshake cups to raise the thirty-five-dollar bail money. "That became so rampant in 1954 and 1955 that particular crowd of dancers, most of whom are in the Shaggers Hall of Fame, finally got fed up. They migrated to Ocean Drive," Thompson said.

THE MYSTIQUE OF O.D.

Trailing calabash fragrances, Highway 17 leaves North Carolina to plunge straight into shag country. Highway 17 cosigns with Highway 9, which connects with Ocean Boulevard. Ocean Boulevard traverses that stretch of beach that continues to define shag's heartland. You can drive up and down the Atlantic Seaboard all you want, but you'll see only one beach where a silhouetted couple shags on a water tower: Ocean Drive.

O.D. had the original O.D. Pavilion, where people danced on Saturday nights. For a dime each, people from Loris in South Carolina and Tabor City and Shallotte in North Carolina, as well as other locales, jitterbugged and waltzed to tunes from a piccolo, another word for jukebox.

Places such as Harley Joe's, Roberts Pavilion, and Sonny's sprang up, and O.D. became a carnival of sorts sequestered among the cottages. A tiny resort, as shagger Gene Laughter wrote, O.D. provided a "summer gathering place for kids who came each summer for a season of sunning, beer drinking, fighting, loving, dancing, hell raising, hustling, and fun." Beach patios and pavilions, dim and "beachy" places, ushered in the glory years, and Ocean Drive reigned as the capital of the shag nation.

Johnie Davis in *Livin' Out Loud* magazine (with permission from Nancy Hall Publications) claims that the music started in Carolina Beach but that O.D. benefited more from it. Or did Carolina Beach dancers migrate to O.D. as Thompson claims?

"In the late 1950s, when Cherry Grove and Ocean Drive had places like the Pad and Sonny's Pavilion, the highway system from the inland cities made travel to O.D. easier than to Carolina Beach. It got real popular down there, but the music started here. It was old blues music," said Davis, whose club still dances to the old blues tunes, not the newer beach tunes. "We dance to 'These Blues is Killing Me' by the Ravens, 'Juke Box' by Gene Pitney, and 'Shut Yo Mouth' by BB King."

Nights at O.D. would begin to sizzle around 10 o'clock. Soon the dance floor was packed, and the iconoclasts of dance commenced another night of legend making.

Deep affection for the day's black rhythm and blues would lead to the proverbial fountain of youth. Shaggers feel they will never grow old because beach music is in their soul. Beach music and shagging created a lifestyle of eternal youth, a time of perpetual summer. Certain words symbolize those glorious days of misspent youth. If you have to ask why these words matter, you're not in the cult.

Beach bums, beach music, drapes, jukebox, magnolias and peaches, O.D., pavilion, PBR, PJ, R&B, race music, the basic, on the beach, the scent of popcorn, French fries, cotton candy, the metallic pop of a cold beer opening, the rhythmic

"SIXTY-MINUTE MAN"

Billy Ward and Rose Marks formed the Dominoes to rival the Ink Spots and Orioles and cross over into the white market. Many radio stations banned this song because of its racy lyrics. This, the first double-entendre record, became the shaggers' anthem.

Photograph by Robert Clark. Courtesy of Harvey and Selene Graham, owners, 94.9 "The Surf" radio.

fall of surf—these words and images do more than create a litany of sorts for members of the shag cult. They resurrect shag's golden days at Ocean Drive, the land of taboo music where the dancing changed.

Sumner Waite, a jitterbugger, went to Ocean Drive in August 1950, and was he in for a surprise. In a 1986 *Carefree Times* there was a letter written by Waite to the editor, which read: "I was a late-blooming teenager, interested in photography and I thought I danced the jitterbug pretty good. I'd learned how on the West Coast one summer. So, I got to O.D. anticipating a fun summer vacation. Well, it didn't take me long to find out my dance style didn't fit Ocean Drive's."

Morning, afternoon, and night Waite hung out at the pavilion, watching the shag and taking pictures. Toward the end of his two-week stay a girl took pity on him. She taught him the basic and the pivot turn.

"From then on," wrote Waite, "there was no way to go but up! I discovered shaggin' was a lot more fun and more complicated than the jitterbug. The summer of 1950 was special. Ocean Drive introduced me to people living in a rustic, carefree environment I hadn't known before."

Waite and many others had found their calling. And in 1951 they found their anthem. A black group, the Dominoes, released what would be a shag anthem, "Sixty Minute Man," one of the first rhythm and blues songs to cross over and climb the popular charts. Written by Billy Ward and Rose Marks, the tune is one of rock and roll's great songs of consequence. To this day the song tops many lists of the greatest beach music songs (see Appendix B). Ward and Marks had put the group together to rival other black groups beginning to win acceptance with white audiences.

Along Ocean Drive in clubs with names such as the Barrel, the Spanish Galleon, and the Myrtle Beach Pavilion, shagging electrified crowds while mortifying the genteel.

An iconic photograph graces the cover of 'Fessa John Hook's *Shagging in the Carolinas*. Sepia-toned and radiating energy, it portrays Leon Williams and a lean-legged woman dancing the dirty shag on Roberts Pavilion's back deck circa 1947. All eyes are riveted on the dancers. One woman's hand has flown over her mouth—appeal and revulsion in one fell swoop. The rebels were loose.

Move over plovers and terns; here comes a new breed of beach wildlife. As O.D. zoomed from a small settlement to a party boomtown, shaggers would party hard, but one breed of wildlife would outdo them all.

THE BEAVER BOYS

O.D. hosted a fraternity in the early 1950s, the Beaver Boys. While it's easy to jump to a conclusion upon hearing this racy nickname, it doesn't mean what you think. No, the lifeguard brotherhood worked for Walter Beaver. Rebellious and hailing from various southern colleges, the Beaver Boys shared interests in black music, pranks, girls, partying, and raising hell. And they never saw a candle they couldn't burn at both ends.

Experienced lifeguards earned thirty-five dollars a week, lived in Beaver's house, and made 10 percent commissions on Beaver's float and umbrella rentals. New lifeguards made twenty-five dollars a week. Many lifeguards moonlighted to squirrel away money for college.

The movie *Animal House* had nothing on the Beaver Boys. They were rowdy, and they commanded respect. Being a lifeguard was prestigious. Throngs of young men wanted to be lifeguards, but few could tolerate the insanity. The partying and pranks never let up.

The cover of the fall 1985 S.O.S. program sports a grainy black and white photo of one of the Beaver Boys in his pith helmet and lifeguard attire teaching Walter Beaver to dance. It's surreal, frozen in time, and Beaver looks ill at ease.

Laughter wrote that Walter Beaver would tire of the shenanigans and threaten to replace the boys with "college Joe types" from his hometown of Kannapolis. According to Laughter, "He would normally back up his threats by bringing down one or two of these colorless drones. They would hardly blend in with other Beaver Boys and could only endure a couple of weeks of our creative pranks before packing for K-town, never to be heard from again."

Laughter laid out the drill that the lifeguards went through each day: "The day started with a wake-up call by Beaver in his slow, nasal twang. This seldom worked and it would take tugs and shoves to get us out of bed and going. After suiting up (white pith helmet, swimming trunks, T-shirt, and whistle around the neck), it was a half-sleep, zombie march to Beaver's shell of an old Dodge and a silent ride down the beach. Beaver would stop at each lifeguard's stand to drop off a hung-over Beaver Boy, who would stumble out and disappear over the sand dunes."

After work the Beaver Boys would meet at Roberts Pavilion for a beer-chugging ritual. After a couple of quarts of Black Label, it was back to Beaver's

SPIVEY'S PAVILION

A rusty pipe—that's all that remained, according to eyewitnesses, after Hurricane
Hazel destroyed Spivey's Pavilion, seen here as if sea mists cover the lens.
Photograph courtesy of Ellen Taylor.

house to shower and dress for an evening of partying with men and women
headed for Roberts Pavilion, Sonny's Pavilion, and Myrtle Beach's Spivey's
Pavilion.

The pavilions were ordinary but exalted. In the early 1980s a writer for
the *Greenville Piedmont,* Melissa Williams, described Spivey's as "a ramshackle,
tattle-tale gray, paint-chipped pavilion." It was an old haunt where people
carved their names in wooden booths overlooking the dance floor. "It was
their domain, where engulfed by friends, their music, and their self-designed
lifestyle, they could revel in rebellion."

Spivey's Pavilion gave new life to what had been a tobacco warehouse in
Aynor. The pavilion became a center of activity for a summer community of
cottages that sprang up near it. It had a jukebox, and there dancers of all ages
took part in the latest crazes: the Big Apple, the Little Apple, the jitterbug, and
then what would become the state dance—the shag.

Roberts Pavilion loomed large in fame and size. It stood where the O.D.
Pavilion stands but was much larger—two stories tall. It was *the* hangout

during the 1940s and early 1950s. A lot of shaggers lived upstairs at Roberts, sharing accommodations.

PEGGED PANTS, PENNY LOAFERS, AND PUMPS

It was late summer 1952. A standing-room-only audience peered through drifts of cigarette smoke at shadowy dancers who moved like ghosts. An ocean breeze cooled the sultry dancers. The Clovers' doo-woppish "Ting a Ling" rocked the floor. Men, dubbed peacocks because of their fancy ways, executed embellished dance steps while wearing pleated, pegged, baggy pants referred to as "drapes," ornate but tasteful. The pants along with penny loafers (no socks), shirtless V-neck cashmere sweaters or button-down oxford shirts, and peroxided ducktail hair identified the beach fraternity—a cult of tight-knit rebels.

You could determine where a beach cat came from by the design of his "pegs." How ironic that they were called beach bums; they wore the most expensive, tailored threads of the day. Any beach cat worth his sea salt would be seen only wearing his tailored pegs.

NO SOCKS ALLOWED

David "Nite Train" Lane's famed shoes, "Weejuns," get their name from "Norwegian." This moccasin-style shoe first appeared in Norway in the mid-30s. G. H. Bass made them in the United States in 1934. Weejuns' tassels inspired Phil Sawyer's column in *Carefree Times*.

Photograph by Robert Clark.

Peg pants were twenty inches at the knee and tapered down to fifteen inches at the cuff. A shop in Wilmington, North Carolina, in 1944 and 1945 made tailored clothes. Jim Hanna, the first fellow on the beach with draped pants, got a pair there with sixteen-inch bottoms, twenty-eight-inch knees, half-inch open-welt seams on the sides, up-flapped pockets on the back, quarter-cut pockets in the front, and belt loops dropped an inch from the top of the waistband.

Dancers meticulously planned their wool or flannel pants, rendered in shades of brown, blue, or gray. Dancers added their fashion statements to the beach life culture of the 1940s and 1950s. It wasn't unusual either to see a casual shagger walking the beach in a white V-neck T-shirt with cigarettes tucked snugly in a rolled sleeve.

"Drapes" describes how the pants hung, and the term captures their purpose: to veil the dancer's leg movements. Sporting peroxided ducktails, blond-ish males with Chesterfields in hand gave the crowd what it came to see: a performance.

And so did the girls. Women in tight, curve-clinging shorts responded to the peacocks' lead with the basic, flawlessly punctuating the music's rhythm, perfectly mirroring their partners. Often they wore pleated, mid-length skirts; pumps or penny loafers with heavy white socks; silk scarves around their necks; and jaunty hairstyles. Some wore bebop shoes and shoes referred to as "elfies." In the 1950s they sported the "sweater and skirt" look. Some had bodies qualifying them as femme fatales, and they dressed to kill.

The showy males kept haberdashers busy—too busy perhaps. A 1982 S.O.S. newsletter "looking-back piece" described how dancers tried to outdo each other: "Pegs evolved into a parody. Extremism prevailed. Flaps became grotesque cancers. Buttons popped up everywhere. Like the dinosaur, pegs became overspecialized. The end came swiftly during the summer of 1954. Strong winds caught the oversized two-inch open welt seams of three beach cats at Roberts Pavilion and hurled them far out to sea into the Bermuda Triangle. The wonderful era of pegs had ended and so had beach individuality."

Thanks to pegs, peerless performances, and more, O.D. assumed a mystique that lives on today. If you shagged, you were a rebel. The glory was yours. If you loved beach music, you would never want for friends who shared your lifestyle. In the minds of many shaggers, "cult" defines this way of life. Jimmy Buffet has his parrotheads, and beach music has its shaggers, a sect that sprang forth from carefree summer life in those glorious days of youthful abandon.

FAT HAROLD'S ON THE BEACH

For many latter-day shaggers their first "beach music" experience took
place in this hallowed old club that was razed September 19, 1988.

Photograph by Bill Kelly. Courtesy of Phil Sawyer.

THE SWITCH

The shag capital assumed a new identity in 1968, North Myrtle Beach. However, a trace of sea salt and coconut oil in the air, a glimpse of a shell necklace,
and the opening notes of a certain song turn shaggers' thoughts not to North
Myrtle Beach but to Ocean Drive. What a shame the name changed from O.D.
to N.M.B. O.D. embraces something a bit larger: fame. More than a few shaggers miss the fabled name. Said Wayne Bennett of the Golden Isles Shag Club,
"I'm nostalgic. I still refer to Ocean Drive as O.D. when talking shag to my
friends. It will always be O.D. to me."

Bennett draws from a well of memories. He said, "I grew up in Delaware
and naturally didn't know what 'Beach Music' was." He took a trip to Ocean
Drive and fell in love. "After that trip to O.D., I knew I had been born a South-
erner and wished I had grown up in the South. Fat Harold's on the Beach
was the club we visited that June evening and, of course, the O.D. Pavilion. I

ALL SHAG ROADS LEAD TO OCEAN DRIVE.

Shaggers signed this old signpost, now at Fat Harold's, in the late 50s.
Look closely. Recognize any names from the glory days?

Photograph by Robert Clark.

remember having my first spodiodie there. Best experience of my late teen years."

David Jones of the Sumter Shag Club had a similar perspective. "It will always be Ocean Drive or O.D. to me and many others who have been around for a while," he said.

Tim Hauser, president of Brushy Mountain Shag Club in North Wilkesboro, North Carolina, said, "O.D. will always be where the heart of shagging resides."

Stacy Marshall, Raleigh Shag Club president, had this to say: "If you change the name you change the history. Look at all the artists who have sung songs about it."

"Many of the old shag songs have shagging on Ocean Boulevard," said Marcia Conway, Northern Virginia Shag Club president." Changing the name left the songs without a home.

O.D. drew dancers. They came from small towns, spots in the road, rural areas, and cities: Charlotte; Columbia; Savannah; Charleston, South Carolina;

SMOOTH STEPS, SMOOTH FLOORS

Song after song, grain against grain, shaggers' shoes wore old plywood floors smooth, creating a look akin to an aerial of desert dunes.

Photograph by Robert Clark.

Charleston, West Virginia; Fayetteville; Greensboro; Florence—throughout the Pee Dee and beyond.

In shag land all roads lead to O.D. for a simple reason. That's where the magic began. "O.D." describes both the place and shaggers' habit—overdosing on dance.

Kay Hatcher grew up just outside Lumberton, North Carolina. For her, a trip to Ocean Drive meant a drive of about an hour and fifteen minutes. For most of her life she's felt the dance's pull.

Hatcher said, "I became addicted to shagging. My memories as a teenager are of being able to scoot to the beach for a Friday or Saturday night date. I remember dancing on those old plywood floors with the salty beach air blowing my hair. Most of the places in those days were open air and the floors were gritty with sand. Somehow, checking for being 'of age' didn't seem to matter so much then. I guess we were more responsible and a little less rowdy than today's teens. So we were able to enter the bars without much questioning, although I did not even drink as a teen. I was the perfect designated driver."

Hatcher remembers dancing at Fat Jack's as a teenager and college-age young lady. She remembered, "Most of the dance places had plywood, sand gritty floors, so the suede-bottomed shag shoes of today would have taken quite a beating. We danced and sweated in the open-air bars with no AC, with the beach breeze blowing all around us. I guess in those days we didn't even have AC in many of our homes, so it didn't matter. We just knew we were happy making friends and enjoying the great music."

THE PAVILIONS

Linda (Burress) Joyce remembers how O.D. became a sanctuary before the switch. "There was no North Myrtle Beach back then. We all knew it as Ocean Drive. I am originally from Sumter, and the first beach we went to was Pawley's Island; this was around 1957. It had a great pavilion (Lafayette) built over the marsh," she said.

Linda and some girls would go several times a summer and shag at the pavilion. The Lafayette pavilion burned down, and Linda and her friends moved to Ocean Drive to shag.

The old pavilions provided a lot of rough-hewn allure. William Roberts built his pavilion in 1936. This early open-air, oceanfront pavilion operated in O.D. to 1954. Its jukeboxes played post–World War II rhythm and blues, as did other popular pavilions on the beach. Hurricane Hazel sent Roberts Pavilion

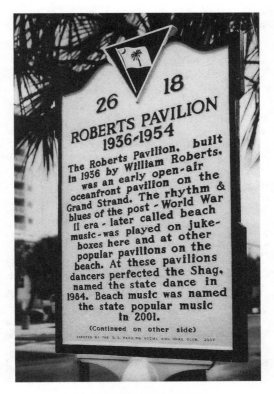

ROBERTS PAVILION MARKER

Photograph by Robert Clark.

into the annals of beach music history, and the Ocean Drive Pavilion was built from salvaged timbers in 1955–57 on the old foundation.

N. F. Sonny Nixon built Sonny's Pavilion in Cherry Grove. It too was an open-air pavilion. Nixon started out with a small gazebo. In 1947 he added a jukebox and then built his pavilion in 1949. While Ocean Drive had a strict midnight curfew for its clubs, Cherry Grove did not. Hardcore shaggers who liked dancing to dawn loved Sonny's Pavilion. Hazel destroyed it too in 1954, but Nixon rebuilt it in 1955. It remained popular with shaggers but became a family arcade during shag's dark ages in the 1970s. Hurricane Hugo put Sonny's Pavilion out of its misery in 1989.

Four beach pavilions stood at or close by North Ocean Boulevard and Ninth Avenue from 1902 to 2006. They were built by the Burroughs & Chapin

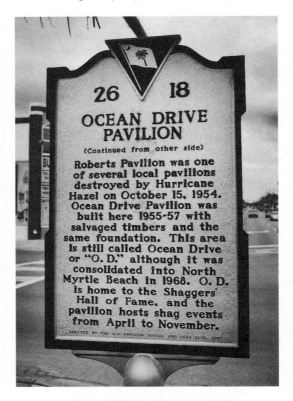

OCEAN DRIVE PAVILION MARKER

Photograph by Robert Clark.

Co. or the Myrtle Beach Farms Co. The first, a simple oceanfront shelter, was built in 1902. The second, built in 1907, was a frame building one and a half blocks from the beach. The third pavilion, a two-story frame structure, went up in 1923 but burned in 1944. A two-story concrete pavilion replaced it in 1949. Its "Magic Attic" hosted bands and other acts, and its jukebox, of course, played rhythm and blues. The wrecking ball took it down in 2006.

Vicki Chaffin described how one old pavilion retains the magic formula of years past: "Our beloved OD Pavilion stands at the site of the old Roberts Pavilion. The 'Pav' might be the last open air shag venue with the beach almost touching the dance floor. The balmy ocean breezes blow onto the dancers and our view is the Atlantic."

It was a setting perfect for fun, classic dancers, and romance. To this day Chaffin reminisces, as others do, about how Billy Jeffers influenced the shag, just as Chicken Hicks influenced the music. Chaffin said, "Jeffers roamed O.D. in the late 1930s. Both men are gone but their memories live on, and in a strange way, they live on too, just as O.D. lives on." Chaffin continued, "One of my most cherished photos is a photo of me dancing with Billy, probably in the early 1990s."

Other clubs existed. Peggy Ann Wrenn recalls the old Cabana Terrace Motor Inn (C.T.), which sat on the oceanfront. It had a lounge overlooking the Atlantic. The Drifters and the Tams played there. This popular landmark never reopened after Hurricane Hazel. Such did the old haunts get blown away; their magical memories are all that remain of their time at O.D.

And O.D.? You can't spell good times without O.D., and good times aplenty were had there. They mound up, a heap of sun-burnished days and moon-struck nights that reign as unforgettable, luminous times. One old shag haunt turned the tables on this story of destruction, ascending from the rubble to legend before it too succumbed to destiny.

Want to blast the dust off old memories? Walk up to a gathering of old beach bums and shaggers and say two words: "the Pad."

BILLY JEFFERS, "THE MAN"

Some people point to Billy Jeffers as the man who "invented" the shag. He dropped the tempo of the swing music, and when he took the floor, the crowd backed off to watch.

Photograph courtesy of Ellen Taylor.

5

The Pad

A land without ruins is a land without memories—
a land without memories is a land without history.

Abram Joseph Ryan,
"A Land without Ruins"

Exactly 262 days after Hurricane Hazel destroyed Ocean Drive on October 15, 1954, the legendary Pad arose on July 4, 1955, from Hazel's rubble. The story behind its ascent to legend is itself worthy of a book.

Henry B. Martin graduated from the University of South Carolina in June 1955. Having spent three years in the Air Force ROTC at USC, Martin had made arrangements to join the U.S. Army in September 1955. With his wife expecting their first child and with no money and no insurance, Martin needed a job. Since he had worked at the beach the three summers before, heading to the coast was an easy decision.

Martin's first stop was in O.D. at a small realty shop operated by C. W. Blankenship, who owned a home a mile down the boulevard with an efficiency apartment attached to it. Martin rented the efficiency for fifteen dollars a week. Blankenship showed Martin a building across from the Ocean Drive Pavilion. An old carport that Blankenship had closed in housed beachcombers in two upstairs units. Downstairs there was a 10 x 20 foot pine-paneled room

THE PAD

Regal in a rustic way, the Pad wore graffiti, frat signs, and names with
grace. Inside was the heart. A cold Budweiser and a hot date dancing
to Fats Domino's "Poor Me" was a slice of heaven on earth. Add a '55
Thunderbird, and it didn't get any better than that.

Courtesy of Becky Stowe.

where someone had operated a small cola, cracker, and cigarette stand. Its saving grace was two pinball machines.

Blankenship made Martin a deal: he'd stock the inventory, and Martin
could operate it. They'd split the profits 50–50. Martin was tired and looking
for a way to cover the next few months' bills. Martin took the deal; trashed
the old, stale inventory; and restocked the place and waited for business. And
he waited and waited. Business was bad save for the pinball machines. What
money he took in he placed in a cigar box, which he kept in the refrigerator.

Every day lifeguards would stop and ask why he didn't sell beer. A dance
floor would be nice too, they said. Put in a jukebox and cut a hole in the wall
and sell beer from the snack place. Suggestions kept coming; income didn't.
Then another one of those shag moments transpired. Next door two men had
just wrapped up laying cement for a Putt-Putt. They were going to throw away
the 2 x 4s they had used as forms for the golf holes. Martin rescued the warped

boards; got a dime-a-play, three-plays-a-quarter jukebox; and put a 25-watt bulb in the one available receptacle. He cut a square hole by the refrigerator and attached hinges so the door would swing.

A day or so later Martin helped a carpenter build a 12 x 12 foot dance floor from old lumber. He got a beer license and was in business. All Martin needed was a name. Tommy Elramey, a lifeguard, suggested that he call it "the Pad," explaining that a popular place in Raleigh had that name. Elramey and Martin built a crude sign from rough-hewn boards and posts that Blankenship bought. Elramey painted "The Pad" on both sides, and the men hauled in sand and sawdust to cover the earthen floor areas.

With the July 4th weekend fast approaching, they filled the refrigerator with Blatz and Miller beer. "Before the paint was dry on the lattice," said Martin, "The 'Pad' came quickly alive." The cold beer went fast, and people drank hot beer straight from the case. "The music played loud from Thursday night through Sunday morning boosted by quarters and the frenzy of a dance called the 'shag,'" said Martin. Martin's much-appreciated take from the jukebox alone was thirty-six dollars.

FROM RUINS COMES A LEGEND

Many a teen had their first taste of Blatz beer at the Pad, and word of mouth from the summer beach workers got the news out. The legend commenced. Martin in time would leave to keep his military commitment, going to Camp Gordon in Augusta, Georgia, and Elramey took over. One postscript merits mention: during all his time at the Pad, Henry Martin never drank a beer. He never sold beer again, nor did he ever learn to shag.

The Pad and O.D. became so intertwined that shaggers could hardly utter a sentence about either without mentioning the other. Yet the Pad was minimalist at best as shag venues went. Bryan's *Shag, the Dance Legend* gives an account of the legendary Pad's beginnings and character.

"The jukebox sat on a sheet of plywood. Cold beer was passed through a hole in an exterior wall. The dancers lounged on junk car seats probably gleaned from the hurricane's wreckage," wrote Bryan. He said that the Pad possessed the earmarks of a first-rate rhythm-and-blues clubhouse, with "scaling paint, low ceilings; the dance floor was upgraded to wooden planks that sagged when the crowd got thick."

"Before the Pad" and "after the Pad" were how many shaggers dated their arrivals at O.D. Bryan wrote that "in North and South Carolina, the Pad gained a recognition factor as high as McDonald's Golden Arches or Holiday Inn's

LEGENDS ALL

The "Queen of Shag," Clarice Reavis and shag pioneer Billy Jeffers face
Jo Jo Putnam at the Pad. This hole in the wall had a hole in the wall that
served up Blatz and Miller beer and something else: fame and memories.

Photograph courtesy of Becky Stowe.

'Great Sign.' Almost no one in the region who achieved the legal drinking age
of eighteen could fail to hear of it."

To be fair, it should be mentioned that other areas had infamous institutions. Jim Crouch Jr. of Gibsonville, North Carolina, remembers another shabby
shag joint, the Sugar Shack, a Chapel Hill institution that provided many
fond memories from his freshman year, 1967–68, at the University of North
Carolina. According to Crouch, "The floor in the main room was dirt and
had the stump of a large tree in the middle. The stump was about 48 inches
in diameter and attempts to smooth it out were only somewhat successful."

As for legalities and protocol, in keeping with shaggers' fondness for their
favorite adult beverage, they were pretty easy to get around. In addition, of
course, music—the sine qua non—was ever present.

BLANKENSHIP'S CLOSED-IN CARPORT

What began as a Coke, cigarette, and cracker joint became a venerable
old jump joint named after a popular Raleigh nightspot. Its first operator,
Henry B. Martin, ironically neither drank beer nor learned to shag. Before
it closed, the Pad was last used as a Halloween haunted house.

Courtesy of Penny M. Herzog.

"A young man could get a beer if he had his junior high library card,"
said Crouch. "The jukebox blared the songs of the '60s, but I don't remember
much dancing because it was usually so crowded. It was paradise for freshman
men, because some of the older sorority girls were in attendance. The views
were spectacular!"

Crouch, alluding to another shag joint, can't be sure, but he thinks the
Sugar Shack closed during his junior year, 1969. He said, "Maybe we just quit
going there because we didn't want to get dust on our Weejuns. Clarence's
offered a better venue, as it had a linoleum floor!"

The Pad had no linoleum, but it had personality. Bryan referred to Ocean
Drive as a sleepy village whose identity was hijacked by the Pad. He reported,
"At times, the crowds were so thick, the dancers only had room to hold hands
and shuffle. The empty beer cans piled up like drifting snow, knee deep in the
corners. Behind the bar, the ice used to hold the beer turned to tepid water

THE OCEAN FOREST HOTEL

Big bands played on the Marine Patio, where people danced ragtime
style beneath the stars in the '50s. When the evening show closed,
bands would go "over the hill" to Charlie's Place and play.

Postcard courtesy of Ellen Taylor.

from the body heat. After ten o'clock at night it was impossible to buy a cold
brew, and so the dancers drank it hot."

The crowds were perceived as "a public nuisance, an affront to civil dignity
and a traffic hazard." Back then O.D.'s chief of police, Merlin Bellamy, "the
Wizard," arrested more kids on the sidewalk in front of the Pad than the jail-
house could hold. "That thing kept me going to court back and forth all the
time," said Bellamy.

As Bryan put it, "spending the night slammed down in the Ocean Drive
drunk tank became a rite of passage, a sort of 'must have' experience. Bellamy
wasn't as bad as some made out and many years later he'd say of the Pad, 'If an
old building could talk, the Pad certainly could tell the tale . . . that building
withstood enormous crowds, rats, and even Hurricane Hazel. I was hung in
effigy there.'"

Bellamy would ask an apparent vagrant where he was staying. Often the
reply was, "At the Ocean Forest," an exclusive hotel of the day. "What they
meant," said Bellamy, "was they stayed in the ocean by day and the forest by

THE KMAS

The Knights of Many Abilities (or Adventures), or simply
Kiss My Ass, had a sanctuary at the Pad, a back room with
mattresses where they no doubt rested, ahem.

Photograph by Robert Clark.

night." Bellamy was chief of police, garbage man, and fire chief all rolled into one. "Some of the young boys who were arrested on trivial matters were sentenced to work on the garbage truck," said Bellamy.

Few knew Bellamy better than the irreverent in-crowd, the Knights of Many Abilities or Many Adventures, or the K.M.A.s. A back room at the Pad with mattresses provided these elitists a sanctuary of sorts. Bryan said, "Only the knights and certain damsels of extreme coolness were allowed to lounge there. The K.M.A.s were the barons of cold beer and beach fever. And to the cops and to the touristy spectators, those unlucky, unwashed souls who could neither dance nor exhibit a proper suntan, the K.M.A.s were the knights of 'kiss my ass.'"

FROM THE RUBBLE of Hurricane Hazel the Pad arose phoenixlike to create many, many memories. Talk to veteran shaggers, and it doesn't take long before certain venues dominate the conversation. The Pad is one such place.

DANCIN' IN THE PAD

Carl and Ellen Taylor dancing. All dancers watch their feet with purpose.
Note the West Virginia chrome holding the wiring in place.

Courtesy of Ellen Taylor.

Few photographs of the venerable Pad exist. As one shagger put it, "We reserved our quarters for beer and the jukebox. No one had money for a camera, film, and all that."

There's one photo, however, of the Pad that portrays dancers in their element. Aged and marred by time, the photograph nonetheless captures the simple joys found at this revered dump. One fellow stands near the latticework, Budweiser and cigarette in hand. The man next to him watches a brunette's footwork. The dancers study their feet. In the middle of it all, Carl and Ellen Taylor dance beneath an electric wire secured to a wooden support by West

Virginia chrome. Other couples fill the frame in this club where you plastered your name over its beams and walls or risked being a nobody.

Nothing much special happened here. Just a lifetime of memories.

HANGIN' AT THE PAD

Forbidden fruit—the taste tempts many. Perhaps it was the rough fellows who hung out there. Perhaps it was the prospect of love at too tender an age. Hanging out at the Pad looking for love was a "must have" experience a lot of parents and others didn't want their kids to have. The Pad posed a hazard to tender kids, causing their parents and in some cases grandparents to intervene. That was the case for Malinda Rutledge-Carlisle.

The Rutledge name is well known throughout South Carolina. Brothers John and Edward played key roles in this country's birth. Edward signed the Declaration of Independence, and John signed the Constitution. Malinda descended from the line originating with John Rutledge. She, like so many others, remembers the Pad as taboo.

"It was off limits to those of us who grew up in the 1960s and wanted to go there," said Malinda, who has lots of "sneak out" stories about the Pad. "There was a drop point at Ocean Drive where we'd sneak around and try to get in."

In a touch of irony the off-limits Pad flaunted a large sign that boasted, "Boogie in the Pad Cause Yo Momma Did." That sign undercut many a mother's admonition.

Malinda was too young to get in. She said, "I had a boyfriend who would come down the same week every August and our big night out was to walk by the Pad and wish we could get in . . . we were not 18." And so they settled for walking to the O.D. Pavilion and hanging around outside the fence drinking cold Pepsis from the drugstore that backed up to the Pad.

She recalls with fondness the haunts she frequented: the Beach Club where Doug Clark and Hot Nuts were the group to see and, of course, sneaking out from the house party her mother was chaperoning to catch tantalizing glimpses of the Pad. Malinda related, "We went in a Model-T truck that one of my best friend's boyfriend, Sandy Barnes of Rock Hill, had. He'd drive up Highway 17 when it was two lanes all the way. Those were the best of times."

Malinda's friend Jane Powell, who dated Barnes (later they married), referred to Highway 17 as "Highway No-No" because of where it led: to "shag country" and that evil Pad.

"Anonymous source close to the jukebox" remembers this off-limits, scruffy venue. "Some of my Rock Hill friends' families had beach houses or business there, so I got to tag along," she said. Anonymous worked "on the beach" the summer after graduating from high school in 1965. "Finally I went into the forbidden territory of the Pad and heard the Tams, live."

Linda (Burress) Joyce treasures a relic from those days, an original business card from the Pad; she said, "I wrote my name all over the Pad, like everyone else did." She recalls too the friendly "keeping up with the Joneses" on the Pad's dance floor. "Back then, the guys would make up steps, and the girls would make up steps. This made us even on the dance floor," she explained.

Linda remembers that they stayed close by. "We would always have a group that would rent B-29, the house right behind the Pad. The Blankenships owned it and the Pad. Those were great times and great friends."

As for money, it had a way of disappearing. "My best girlfriend's father had us a charge account at Hardwick's so we would eat right because we were always eating doughnuts and chocolate milk," said Linda. "Sometimes all of our money would go to get boys out of jail."

Don Ray, once the chief building inspector for North Myrtle Beach, remembered one thing about the Pad. "Unless you got handcuffed to a palm tree, you had not yet passed the rites of manhood," he said.

Bailing out the boys—a true sign of friendship. The Society of Stranders' motto of "Good Friends, Good Times, Great Memories" could well be the slogan for the legendary Pad. Those recalling the Pad echo these themes over and over.

Memories of O.D. and venues such as the Pad have lasted for decades. Not even a hurricane could blow them away.

Judy and Joan Bassett grew up in Fairmont, North Carolina, some fifty miles from Cherry Grove, where they spent every summer. Joan remembers Hurricane Hazel, learning to shag, and being chaperoned at Ocean Drive: "We had the last house on the oceanfront at Cherry Grove in 1954 that Hurricane Hazel took. After Hazel, my father found a house that had blown into the trees where Tide Water is now. He brought it down and put a block foundation under it on the second row at 36 Street. We lived there from 1955 to 1960. Our parents got the four Anderson boys and an ex–Arthur Murray dance teacher to teach us to shag in our living room there in 1957 when I was 10."

Joan's half sister, Kay Cameron, and her best friend, Linda Kinlaw, were shagging at the Pad in 1955, so Joan grew up listening to the Platters, the Ink Spots, Nat King Cole, and other black musicians. Joan said, "My mother would take us to OD Pavilion every night, and then we'd go to the Pad and end up at Sonny's Pavilion. She would sit on the bleachers and watch us. Only the older reliable lifeguards could take us home sometimes. We danced in Weejuns and

Papagallos on the oceanfront, which was pretty steamy. I had to glue my spit curls to my face so they wouldn't droop with sweat."

Joan dated the manager of the Pad, Jim Jayroe, one summer, and they would make up steps on Sunday afternoons. "Sunday was called the 'changing of the guards,'" she said, "because a new crop of tourists would come in for the week and you would go down to Sonny's and pick out a dance partner for the week."

Joan reported that back then none of the dancers drank because they couldn't do the intricate steps such as the drop spins and boogey walks if they didn't have good balance and coordination. "Also," she added, "the good shaggers would never ask just any girl to dance, so when you saw someone you wanted to dance with you had to get a 'guy friend' to dance with you so the out-of-town guys would ask you."

THROUGH THE LATTICE

Many people remember the Pad's lattice. In 1956 Charley Holtzclaw's parents took him to Crescent Beach for a week. He found his way to O.D. and watched people shag through the latticework.

"I was holding on," said Charlie, "learning the basic at the tender age of 13. A beautiful 18-year-old lady saw me, took my hand, walked me inside, and began to teach me how to shag. I was in 'hog heaven.'"

Vicki Chaffin remembers that the Pad's privacy lattice kept prying eyes from the street from seeing what was going on inside. That, of course, was "fast dancing," aka shagging. "Jimmy Rick's and the Raven's 'Green Eyes' or 'Drinkin' Wine Spodie-Odie' or 'White Cliffs of Dover' lured you in," said Chaffin. Dancers making their moves on that sandy, nonair-conditioned dance floor cast a spell over onlookers. "It was breathtaking poetry in motion," said Chaffin, "and you'd think, 'Oh, if I could ever look that cool.'"

In the 1960s Vietnam raged. Chaffin has photos from 1969, "when so many of our beach boys had been sent to Vietnam," she said. One photo shows friends on the roof of the Barrel making peace signs. "That's when peace signs were authentic," said Chaffin.

War or not, the partying went on at the Pad. "Most of our evenings," said Chaffin, "didn't begin until around 11:00 P.M. when we waitresses got off work at 10, went home, got decked and dolled and hit the streets for some shagging."

SNO' CONE GIRLS

Crushed ice and flavored syrup cooled beach girls by day. Down on
the beach, pushing a sno' cone cart was a coveted job whose meager
income let shaggers spend a summer "on the beach."

Courtesy of Becky Stowe.

ON THE BEACH

Back in Ocean Drive, if you worked at the beach, you didn't just say you worked
at the beach. "We called it 'On the Beach,'" said Chaffin, who said the coveted
jobs were sno-cone cart pusher, lifeguard, and waitress. Chaffin continued,
"When I was on the beach in the 1960s, I worked at the Hurricane Seafood
House on the waterfront dock at Little River. Everyone had a nickname—girls
and guys. There was Waco, Bucky Dee, Whisper Jet, Go Boy, and others. Gosh,
was life good . . . and still is."

Chaffin remembers how beach legends such as Go Boy and Hornet and
others had signed their names on the Pad's walls, and she recalls the time Chief
Bellamy's "best" tear-gassed the Pad's revelers "when they didn't leave at closing time or some such rubbish." When that news made the *State* newspaper,
her mom, mindful of shagging's "scandalous" image, sent her a clipping at

college, noting, "See, I told you so." "It didn't matter, said Chaffin. "That place was an awesome landmark in O.D. and I was heartbroken when it was torn down. Never again would that corner be the same."

It was at Ocean Drive that Carolina girls gathered to sun and dance. It was at Ocean Drive where boys from North and South Carolina and beyond sought sweet sun-kissed peaches. It was there up on the roof and on the boardwalk where love and memories bloomed. They blossomed in what some would call dives, but that didn't matter. Music, friendship, and memories—best in the world—came to pass at O.D. in places such as the pavilions and the Pad.

Great memories of the Pad abound to this day . . . when we shake the great barrel of time we call history, a few scraps fall free: the ceiling fan no one would dance under; it always looked like it was ready to fall . . . the difficulty in getting into the Pad it was so packed . . . years of listening to how bad the bathrooms were but never a complaint when they served their purpose . . . good deejays and great shaggin' friends. All that described the Pad, and thus it was that these memories and others from Ocean Drive live on to this day.

Like so many kids back then, Milford Powell of Ocean Drive was "on the beach." Early on he ran the projector for the Ocean Drive Theater, where Georgio's Pizza stands today. Then he worked in a bowling alley settings pins for a nickel a person. "It was the worst job I had in my life," said Powell. "People would throw the ball so hard. They'd try to hit you with it."

Powell remembers other dance venues. "Cecil Corebette of the Beach Club booked the most popular acts," he said. Other names he reeled out include Sonny's Pavilion, Spivey's, the Windy Hill Pier, and O.D. Pavilion, and he recalls Tin Top Alley too. The clubs had staggered closing times, which meant that the dancing crowd moved from venue to venue in migrations, a word oh so familiar to shaggers.

"The Pad was open all day long. When it closed, the crowd would go to Sonny's, which was open to 2 A.M. After that the place to go to was Forks Drive In, which was open from 2 A.M. to 6 A.M., the proverbial crack of dawn," according to Powell.

And then disaster struck.

"The Pad caught fire," said Powell. "Some kids had sneaked in there and were maybe smoking. The fire burned a hole in the roof and the city condemned it."

In the *North Myrtle Beach Times* May 10, 1990, edition, Becky Stowe, an O.D. artist, voiced a popular sentiment: "I just hope they leave the Pad. I don't think anyone fully realizes how famous the Pad really is. There are art prints of the Pad in at least half of the U.S. and in parts of Canada. Tourists from all over the world come by my studio and ask, 'Where's the famous Pad?'"

AN ERA ENDS

Demolition arrived in 1994. They tore the Pad down, a solemn occasion. This institution, this shrine was to be no more. It had endured hurricanes, a tear-gas bomb, the famous Easter riot of 1967, and thousands of drunken shaggers before succumbing to fire. It was the place where "Wheel of Fortune" star Vanna White was conceived, and yet it was torn down on January 28, 1994. White, in an interview with the *Sun News,* said, "It's a landmark."

Its hallowed halls held joy and music no more. Tommy Elramey had opened it on July 4, 1955, and now this "nip joint" was destined for some landfill save one board that would end up affixed to Fat Harold's club.

Powell provides a classic tale of the Pad's last rites. He and a gang of boys and girls, quite properly, took out the old urinal, made from one half of an old water heater, and gave it an impromptu memorial service. "It looked awful and smelled awful," said Powell. "I mean it was just nasty. We carried it out back, used it one more time, said a few respectful words, and then we buried it for posterity's sake where it remains to this day."

Not far from where the Pad stood, Lowcountry sands cradle the old urinal. Some nights the full moon traces silver fringes along clouds' edges and cloud shadows race across Ocean Drive. For a fleeting second if you know just where to look, you may see lifeguards standing around the old urinal, shadows from the glory years.

Jan Morris, former chair of the Society of Stranders' Legends Committee, wrote about the Pad's lovers "who decided not to participate in getting 'old.'" The occasion was the 27th Annual Living Legends Invitational Event held May 14 through May 15, 2010, at Fat Harold's Beach Club. "There were the survivors of the 'before Hazel' years, and many more that came after that 1954 hurricane cleared the old landmarks. The 'after Hazel' years are frequently referred to by the next generation of beach buddies as marked by the birth of a place called 'the Pad.'"

The Pad was a place where lifelong friendships and memories were made. Morris referred to its music, dance, and beach lifestyle that bonded those who returned through the years.

The old joint had an inscription on one wall: "I feel the brotherhood. What a feeling." That feeling lives on in the memories of shaggers who loved the old place and its glorious shabbiness.

One Society of Stranders member, Charlotte Moore, remembers what "the life" was like at the Pad, a venue described also as a shag fortress. She said, "I fell in love with the first sounds of beach, boogie, and blues. I found so many acquaintances, life-long friends, and dance partners through the shag world." Like so many shaggers, Moore referred to the shag as more than a dance. "It's a way of life," she said. "I got into 'the life' just in time to dance at 'the Pad.' It looked like a small shack with an outside porch. Inside was a bit dark with an old wood dance floor. The live band that first afternoon was the Sugarbees, playing on the porch. Shorts, swimsuits, sweat and 'suds,' it was a great afternoon."

She recalls a night never to be forgotten, like the image in that old Tichnor Brothers postcard: "I remember that night being like out of a movie . . . going back to the Pad dressed a tad bit sexier. I was dancing and in walked this tall, lanky good-looking guy, dressed in white slacks, black tee, white jacket, and shag loafers without socks. He saw me, asked me to dance, and we danced till they closed. He was a natural Carolina dancer. He walked me back to the beach condo I was sharing with girl friends, kissed me good night, and I never saw him again. Perfectly beautiful time."

A perfectly beautiful time. Somehow those words elegantly apply to the Pad, a scruffy shag venue that lives on in a place called legend.

6

The Dark Ages

A time to weep, and a time to laugh;
a time to mourn, and a time to dance

Ecclesiastes 3:4

The shag was "a warm night with a cold beer and a hot date and no plans for tomorrow," quipped one shagger, and indeed it was. People were shagging all along the southern Atlantic coast in the 1950s. The shag had ridden a tide of rhythm and blues and sparked a surge of youthful exuberance. It was the "in" thing, and people were eager to play a part in that old dirty dance, the shag.

Through the years self-appointed authorities pronounced just about every resort community on the Atlantic Ocean from Virginia Beach to Savannah as the site of the shag's creation. These claims often credited several famed shaggers for sparking the dance's genesis, even going as far as pinpointing the summer it happened. For a long time a debate has raged between North and South Carolinians: which state can rightfully claim the shag as its own?

The truth is, no one person at any one spot or specific time started the shag. Shagging seems to have popped up like so many mushrooms after a rain. If one place has the right to claim it started the shag, it would be Carolina Beach or Ocean Drive, or more sensibly both. The music changed in North

FIRST IN SHAG?

North Carolina's and South Carolina's separate claims to the
shag fuel debate. Both states have ample reason to make it their
official dance. Just where did those first steps take place?

Photograph by Robert Clark.

Carolina and the dance evolved in South Carolina, but that statement could
easily be reversed.

The dance evolved all along the Atlantic coast beaches and was in full
flower by the early 1950s. Shagging also had an established presence on college
campuses by that time. Ocean Drive Beach ascended to become shag's first city
in part because of its near equal distance from Virginia Beach and Savannah,
its proximity to Myrtle Beach, and its emergence as a vacation venue. If not the
shag's cradle, O.D. was its base camp.

The origin debate aside, shaggers knew one thing: conditions in the United
States would get better. They reveled in their youth and the decade of the 1950s,
perhaps the most talked and written about period in modern American history. Social aspects—music, dancing, entertainment, and lifestyles—took on
prominent roles in the 1950s. Life was good; life was cool.

Among the many tidbits served up by Brendan Greaves and Michael C.
Taylor in "Fooled Around and Fell in Love: Beach Music History and Myth"

(in *Vanity of the Vanities*) is the extreme coolness that shaggers displayed. They quote 'Fessa John Hook on the business of being cool: "In the old stories, the great shaggers on the Grand Stand would wear a cashmere sweater on July 4th and dance out on the deck at the Myrtle Beach Pavilion with their sleeves rolled up, and never break a sweat. [Some dancers] could put an open beer on top of their head and do a drop spin and never spill a drop."

Such fabled coolness held allure. With a tempo of 120 beats a minute, shaggers' songs "felt" right when it came to cool dancing. By the mid to late 1950s—shagging's quintessential period—shaggers referred to their dance as "the basic" or "the fas' dance." Regardless of what they called it, the dance obsessed the Grand Strand's young people dancing in beachfront pavilions and local juke joints, what would be called "beach clubs." They danced to beach music greats such as the Drifters (a group of musicians who came and went), the Clovers, and Maurice Williams and the Zodiacs. Williams, a Lancaster, South Carolina, native, cut his teeth on church music, as did some other consequential singers.

The 1950s are often referred to as an era of social revolution. Significant changes took place in every aspect of the way people lived. Therein lay a problem. Shaggers didn't know it, but a young man who also cut his teeth on gospel music was making a reservation for them at the Heartbreak Hotel. Shaggers were about to face banishment at the hands of two unrelated events.

Two even-numbered years, 1954 and 1956, would deal the shag extraordinary setbacks. One year would deliver a catastrophe, the other a cultural phenomenon. In combination these two years plunged the shag and its devotees into a period considered their dark ages.

OCTOBER 15, 1954

One of the twentieth century's worst hurricanes struck the South Carolina/ North Carolina border during the year's highest lunar tide, roaring ashore at high tide just after a full moon. Hurricane Hazel, a category 4 storm, made landfall near Calabash, North Carolina, halfway between Myrtle Beach and Wilmington, destroying every pier along a 170-mile stretch. An eyewitness reported that the storm surge topped 18.5 feet. Some claimed that it climbed 30 feet or more.

Hazel laid waste to Ocean Drive, which lost 450 houses, and the dance clubs weren't spared either. Sonny's Pavilion disappeared. The storm split Roberts Pavilion asunder. The old beach haunts vanished. The storm, an uninvited catalyst, sparked change.

HAZEL KILLED THE SHAG'S PLAYGROUND

This photograph of Hugo's destruction offers a modern-day
glimpse at what Hazel did to Ocean Drive. Hugo finished
off what remained of Sonny's Pavilion in 1989.

Photograph by Robert Clark.

For many people, it was easier to sell their land than rebuild. All of a sudden land was plentiful for commercial development. Outside capital drove a wave of construction and beachfront development thanks to Hazel. Quaintness, a sacrificial lamb, would be slaughtered.

Real estate development swept in, and the winds of change raged. Restaurants sprouted like mushrooms where worn, wooden dance floors once lay. Hotels sprang up. Picturesque places were no more. The laid-back, casual atmosphere of the old clubs gave way to something called progress. Something precious vanished for shag's trailblazers: the revered pavilions. Hazel's winds blew away the sites of their youthful abandon.

Like a solitary tombstone, a historical marker stands where Hazel razed Roberts Pavilion. All that remained were sand and memories. The shaggers' idle but majestic youth ended with Hurricane Hazel. The realities of life came calling. Many shaggers were taking on jobs and families. Middle age was closing in. At the very time their youthful freedom was dying, a vital connection with the past had been severed. The vanquished pavilions were sacred temples, and life without them could not be the same.

The year 1954 spelled the end of the old and the dawn of the new. It was a benchmark year—a dividing line. Spivey's was gone. The front row of the Grand Strand was laid bare. No more endless summers. Another thing, something vital, changed: the music.

Some 760 miles to the west of Ocean Drive, something was happening that, in an ironic twist, would further shut down the shag nation. A shy, young truck driver from Tupelo, Mississippi, walked into Sam Phillips's Sun Records in Memphis to record a song for his mom, though some speculate that he walked into Sun hoping to be discovered. It's easy to see why he chose the Sun recording studio; its slogan helped dispel any nerves: "We Record Anything, Anywhere—Anytime."

"What kind of singer are you," asked Marion Keisker, the receptionist.

"I sing all kinds," said the truck driver.

"Who do you sound like," asked the receptionist.

"Uh, I don't sound like nobody."

This modest but prophetic reply lingered in the receptionist's mind. In the summer of 1954 Sam Phillips, Sun's legendary owner, needed a new kind of singer. The receptionist, struck perhaps by the truck driver's unusual looks, asked Phillips, "Why don't you try that young truck driver?"

The timing was good. Phillips was primed to move into new music territory. Said Phillips, "Everyone knew that I was just a struggling cat down here trying to develop new and different artists, and get some freedom in music, and tap some resources and people that weren't being tapped."

Phillips recognized the power of the blues and signed a lot of black musicians. "They were great untried, unproven people with talent," said Phillips. It dawned on him that they had great talent and great potential but too few recording opportunities. "I knew of their poverty and background because I had lived it. The only difference between me and many of them was my white skin. . . . It was up to me," he said, "to listen to them."

BLACK BLUES AND A WHITE SINGER

Many years after his days at Sun, Phillips served up a telling perspective: "There is nothing greater to do than the blues if you would be a musician. Whether vocally, instrumentally, there is nothing easier yet more difficult; there is no way for anybody to write the essence of the blues as a score. That has to come instantaneously. So much of what is here now is owed to the blues, both black and white. And if you listen to the blackest black cat or the whitest white hill-billy, you're gonna hear something worthwhile. It's a symphony of the soul. There is no question about it."

By the spring of 1954 Phillips had lost his symphony. With the old hard race lines softening, many of his successful black artists had jumped to larger labels. Undeterred, Phillips sought new ways to establish the Sun Records sound. Phillips talked about this musical fork in the road: "I'd been looking for a person, a white-skinned person that could put the feel of a black person into a phonograph record, knowing we grew up in the same fields, so to speak—cotton fields, corn fields, even before we grew soybeans, watermelon patches, whatever—blacks and white. I knew the power of the feel between the races, and I was not interested in forming another record company and trying to compete even with the bigger independents at that time—I had no interest in that if I couldn't broaden the base of music and let white kids enjoy black music and black kids enjoy white music."

The words of the late Sam Phillips should resonate with shaggers. Men like him wanted to open the door to race music. In one of music's great ironies, Phillips would be among the factors that led to the shag's dark ages.

It started with Marion Keisker's suggestion: "Why don't you try that young truck driver?" Suppose she had said, "Well, damn, Sam. What are you going to do?" But she didn't. And so in the summer of 1954 Elvis Presley, that truck driver for the Crown Electric Company, walked into Sun Records yet again, this time to record "Without Love." The reticent truck driver, however, couldn't do "Without Love" justice, disappointing Phillips.

Phillips nonetheless asked the young singer to audition another time with Winfield "Scotty" Moore and bassist Bill Black. Again the audition wasn't working out. Then one of recording's seminal moments arrived on July 5, 1954. The musicians took a break, and the ducktailed singer loosened up while singing "That's All Right, Mama," a song written by Arthur "Pop" Crudup, a delta blues singer and guitarist. Like fog off the Mississippi, the elusive sound Phillips sought materialized right in front of him.

Said Phillips, "I heard this rhythm, just by himself and I said, 'Jesus! Elvis, have you been holding out on me all this time and have cost me this much time?'"

Elvis, seeing Phillips's reaction, said, "You like that, Mr. Phillips?"

"Man, that thing is a hit," said Phillips, "that thing is a hit," and he hustled the musicians into the studio. By the second cut, Phillips knew what he had. Sun released "That's All Right, Mama" as a 78-rpm. Soon it was charting across the South, and the name Elvis Presley began to burn itself into the annals of history.

Elvis's first number one pop record seared his name into the American consciousness. "Heartbreak Hotel" reigned as the number one tune on the Billboard Pop Singles Chart for eight weeks in 1956. Elvis was bringing a second dagger to shag's heart.

By 1957 Elvis Presley was the world's most famous entertainer. A PBS documentary described Presley as "an American music giant of the 20th century who single handedly changed the course of music and culture in the mid 1950s."

How big was Elvis? Big enough to set in motion events that would derail the shag. His influence would cast a long, long shadow across the Atlantic.

Technology was an influence too. It gave a growing teen populace a way to hear "the King." Throngs of American teenagers were scooping up transistor radios and listening to rock 'n' roll. In 1955 one hundred thousand units were sold. By the end of 1958 five million units had sold, but American teens weren't the only ones listening to Elvis's new brand of rock.

ACROSS THE ATLANTIC

Unfettered by segregation and aided by "renegade" radio stations, large numbers of British teens formed bands in the 1950s to imitate their American hero. Elvis's music, moves, attitude, and clothing symbolized rock and roll. He seemed rebellious, an outlier, and he had already paved the way for countless American performers, among them Little Richard, Chuck Berry, Jerry Lee Lewis, the Everly Brothers, Buddy Holly, Roy Orbison, and others who would influence the Brits.

Keith Richards of the Rolling Stones first heard American black music over "blacklisted" Radio Luxembourg, which once boasted the world's most powerful transmitter and broadcast pop music to the British Isles from 1954 to 1963. Then he heard the King.

In *Life*, Richards wrote, "Radio Luxembourg was notoriously difficult to keep on station. I had a little aerial and I'd walk around the room, holding the radio up to my ear and twisting the dial . . . I'm supposed to be asleep. . . . Like an explosion one night, listening to Radio Luxembourg on my little radio was 'Heartbreak Hotel.' That was the stunner. I'd never heard it before, or anything like it. I'd never heard of Elvis before. It was almost as if I had been waiting for it to happen. When I woke up the next day, I was a different guy."

The lads liked what they heard, and they began to form bands and make rock music. It was Elvis more than anyone who influenced the Brits. Years later Radio Luxembourg would be the first European radio to announce Elvis's death.

Said George Harrison, "Seeing Elvis was like seeing the messiah arrive."

John Lennon told Jerry Schilling, one of Elvis's bodyguards, to tell Elvis, "If it hadn't been for him, I would have been nothing."

Paul McCartney recorded "Heartbreak Hotel" using Bill Black's bass at Abbey Road Studios. Said McCartney, "It was Elvis who really got me hooked on beat music. When I heard 'Heartbreak Hotel,' I thought, this is it. Musically it's perfect."

Shaggers weren't enamored of Elvis. Jo Jo Putnam abandoned the beach "when the Ivy League settled in and there wasn't the ambience and charisma like before. Elvis Presley had started his campaign to destroy good music and the old crowd was gone."

Other musical distractions took place. A fellow born in Spring Gulley, South Carolina, Ernest Evans, had a hit song with its own dance craze. Adopting the stage name "Chubby Checker," Evans's "The Twist" did its part to undercut the shag. "The Twist" got adults who refused to dance to "teen tunes" onto the dance floor, but it wasn't to shag.

The assassination of President John F. Kennedy in late November 1963 cut a deep hole into the psyche of the United States, creating a cultural vacuum. It didn't take long for outside influences to fill the vacuum with fresh material.

On February 9, 1964, a defining moment changed everything. The Beatles' historic appearance on "The Ed Sullivan Show" garnered the then-largest television audience in history. This remarkable social and cultural milestone marked the start of the "British Invasion." Releasing a two-year backlog of hits from England, the Beatles dominated the American charts. On April 4, 1964, the Beatles occupied the top five spots on *Billboard* magazine's Hot 100 music survey, a feat unmatched before or since. Such total domination blew away American acts, among them the makers of shag tunes.

In his book *This Magic Moment—Musical Reflections of a Generation,* Harry Turner wrote, "When the British invasion began, my friends and I thought that it was kind of amusing, but we never viewed it as good music. We thought that it would simply be a fad and the R&B-based music that we loved best would re-establish its pre-British Invasion position of strength. Suddenly, R&B, rockabilly, teen idol, folk, popular rock and roll, and other diverse American artists found themselves with one thing in common—they were without recording contracts."

In 1964 a cultural shift was unleashed. If you were in your thirties, you were done: a culture of youth spread across the country like the big bang. Tensions between blacks and whites climbed the charts. The civil rights movement didn't dance to rhythm and blues. It marched and staged "sit-ins."

Then the antiwar protests started. All of this upheaval found its identity in the irreverent personas of the Rolling Stones. Like Elvis, they were white but sounded black. They played American music, via England. In a bizarre twist they dressed much like women. They grew their hair long, and women of all ages and backgrounds desired them.

Other British acts swamped the American music scene. Along came the Dave Clark Five, Gerry and the Pacemakers, Peter and Gordon, the Animals, the Kinks, Manfred Mann, Herman's Hermits, the Zombies, and Petula Clark—all by the end of 1964. Britain seemed to produce wave after wave of bands, most with long hair. American bands were quick to pick up on the look and sound of the British groups. Groups such as the Byrds incorporated the British musical styles, hairstyles, and dress. An endless line of rock bands pushed shag music out the back door. The old music began to die.

THE BRITISH INVASION stimulated the widespread formation of new rock and roll bands in America, similar to what had occurred in the United Kingdom ten years earlier under the influence of American artists. The British Invasion had played out by 1967, but the damage had been done, if you were a shagger. And if you were a newcomer who had yet to hear of the shag, the chances were you wouldn't.

The styles and influences of the British bands had recharged the American rock and roll scene. The British Invasion offered audiences a new model: the self-contained rock group. The solo performer backed by stage or session musicians had fallen out of vogue. Rock acts composed their own tunes. In addition single hits were out. The British acts, led by the Beatles, set a new standard: the high-quality long-playing album as the prime venue for the release of recordings. The popularity of 45-rpms declined, and jukeboxes lost a bit of their dazzle.

The shag, its moon waning, now suffered from a crowd a bit rough around the edges. No explanation exists for this unruliness. Perhaps it was a bit exaggerated. Perhaps it was true. A longtime shagger who prefers to be identified as "an anonymous source close to the jukebox" remembers those days as being a bit disorderly: "Like all South Carolina kids, I got myself to Ocean Drive/Cherry Grove by any legal means during the 1960s. Myrtle Beach was considered a 'rough' place at night and usually full of Yankee tourists and military guys on leave looking for trouble. I never saw a fight but we girls stayed away from potential trouble spots. Some of the best male dancers had reputations as fighters. They were dangerous guys in more than one way."

Unlike "anonymous," fewer and fewer teens took up the shag. Even the most accomplished dancers retreated. The shag had been relegated to a disquieting status: "no longer fashionable." Its bands weren't popular. Its dance wasn't popular, not with the masses. Dancing now consisted of "fast" free-style movement to rock with partners standing apart, often far apart. The graceful symmetry of a couple in the old, wooden pavilions on sandy dance floors had been supplanted by hard-driving rock, and then along came *Saturday Night Fever*. John Travolta starred in the dance movie of the decade, establishing disco as the dance and disco joints as the venues of the in-crowd where glitzy couples danced beneath glittering mirror balls.

From Motown to the Beatles to disco, the shag reeled beneath an assault of cultural change. The venerable culture that had wielded a forever effect on shaggers was disappearing beneath successive waves of new music. To be a shagger was to be an outlier. Shagging remained the dance of those who, in effect, now amounted to a resistance. If you were an old-guard shagger, it was not a time to dance. It was a time to weep.

Many shaggers found themselves to be an enclave of anachronistic outcasts coping as best they could in a dance Hades. They didn't perceive of themselves as old-fashioned, but that's how others saw them. During its heyday, the shag had been "a warm night with a cold beer and a hot date," but life without the shag had become cold, dry, and lonely.

1

A Reunion, a Revival

Some threw rocks. Many wore sandals with tire-tread soles, footwear as far from Weejuns as bell-bottomed jeans were from khakis. And hippies' psychedelic tie-dyed shirts? They were light years from pegged pants and cashmere sweaters. But that's the way it was in the dark ages.

A new cultural wave had swept over America flaunting its brand of irreverence as a different attitude gripped the country. Flower power, peace, love chants, and free sex—in a haze of marijuana smoke—dethroned the nights of cold beers and hot dates. And a lot of folks had plans for tomorrow: demonstrations and dissent.

Vietnam did the shag no favors. The Southeast, at first, had been spared much of the war-time angst, but no region of the country avoided the Vietnam controversy. The nation's mood turned ugly, and carefree shaggers retreated like an army on the run. Shaggers to this day still refer to this period as "the dark ages." And well they should.

The country seemed to hold nothing but depressed souls. The war in Vietnam was not going well, and most everyone knew someone who had lost a friend or family member to the war. Protesters dominated the evening news, and a great rift cleaved the nation into anti- and pro-war factions; in addition the drug culture piled on top of everything.

Timothy Leary's "tune in, turn on, drop out" became the counterculture's mantra, and songs deep in meaning with soul-probing lyrics became its music.

The weed-loving generation danced free form: it had no interest in the smooth, silky moves of the shag.

Woodstock of 1969, the so-called Aquarian Exposition, and long hair supplanted Ocean Drive and ducktails. Anthems such as the Youngbloods' "Get Together" moved the masses. And beach music? It was an old Model T, a Tin Lizzie to be replaced by newer, "with it" models.

In this weighty era endearing lyrics and apolitical music came across to some as fluff. "Give Me Just a Little More Time" was not what protesters wanted to hear. Nor were they interested in strolls by the breakers holding a pretty girl's hand. If shaggers represented innocence, hippies represented the death of innocence, and many, intoxicated as they were with their own youth, viewed shaggers as old fogeys.

In the early 1970s shaggers were scattered, exiled by changing times, relegated to dance prisoners. By the mid-1970s the disco wave had entrenched itself, and it would be propelled around the world in 1977 by the huge commercial success of *Saturday Night Fever,* a movie that made John Travolta a

THE QUEEN OF SHAG

A lover of the blues, Clarice Reavis went to Charlie's Place. On July 13, 2005, three years, six months, two weeks, and one day after she died, the North Carolina General Assembly ratified Fayetteville's Clarice Reavis as the Queen of Shag.

Photograph courtesy of Al and M. G. Cain.

household name. The *Saturday Night Fever* soundtrack, featuring songs such as the Bee Gees' "Staying Alive," became the best-selling soundtrack of all time, but you can't shag to disco.

LANDLOCKED

Shaggers had long gone inland to shag haunts when the beach season ended. Harry Driver remembered traveling in Clarice Reavis's orange Cadillac to any-place Jimmy Cavallo's band was playing. Cavallo, a singer and saxophonist, and his House Rockers played a brand of R&B in 1949 that "let the music loose," according to Bo Bryan, yet another claim as to how beach music began. Driver and Reavis went to Gray's in Dunn-Erwin, the Raleigh Memorial Auditorium, Stewart's Lake in Raleigh, and Breece's Landing in Fayetteville. Reavis, a shapely and smoldering beauty, was the queen of shag, and of her Bryan wrote: "She was strong as train smoke. You take a deep breath, she'd knock you out.'"

Like desperadoes on the run, shaggers proved resilient, migrating inland from the coast. They too were staying alive as the 1970s wound down in pockets where hangers-on hung on keeping shag's embers aglow.

In "Bop 'til You Drop, Shag 'til You Drag," Jim Dodson wrote in *America* magazine in the spring of 1982 that a resurgent interest in beach music took root in Atlanta in 1981. He said, "This so-called new wave of beach music popularity began in Atlanta last year, signaled by the opening of several beach music clubs with names such as Ocean Drive South and Buckhead Beach."

In another capital city, Columbia, South Carolina, several beach clubs would open to fill the void that had for so long gone unfilled. Charlotte and small towns throughout eastern North Carolina had beach clubs too. Most clubs used a familiar formula: cold beer; a collegelike bar atmosphere; and beach music recorded by the Platters, the Tams, and the Drifters.

Among the winds keeping the embers aglow were dance contests that came about in a chance manner. Bryan in *Shag* captured a key moment in 1973 that played a role in popularizing the dance contests. Shaggers Shad and Brenda Alberty accepted a friend's invitation to join him at a Charlotte Ramada Inn bar. "'The dance floor was about the size of a cocktail table,' Brenda remembered. For Brenda Alberty, the fever had never died. 'I would have to stop myself from wanting to go to the beach so badly.'"

During the summer of 1973 the Albertys went to Atlantic Beach, North Carolina, for a vacation. They had heard that a bar there still played the real McCoy rhythm and blues. That place was called the Jolly Knave.

According to Bryan, "The Jolly Knave was a rough-sawn joint, reminiscent of the old pavilions. It sat on the waterfront with a wide deck overcooling the beach. The Albertys ended up at the Jolly Knave that summer where they danced to Wynonie Harris's 'Shake That Thing.' A hush fell across the crowd. The Albertys' dancing transported onlookers back to the days of forbidden music and dancing fraught with risks. It was one of those magical moments people realized they should repeat over and over if at all possible."

The Jolly Knave's proprietor asked the Albertys how other dancers could get together. Dance contests surfaced as possible ways. The Jolly Knave held a dance contest, and as Bryan wrote, "On the afternoon of the competition, the joint was so crowded people climbed into the rafters, drank beer, and ogled the performers like monkeys from the treetops."

Other contests popped up, and week after week a competitive dance fire raged. Five years sped by, during which time a professional dance circuit arose. Shaggers were a step closer to being organized even though neither organizations nor shag clubs existed . . . yet.

As the 1980s approached, renewed interest in shagging and beach music kept the embers aglow. Beach music was transitioning from sporadic, spontaneous occasions to organized events. Contests were here to stay. Bands gave way to deejays, who emerged as keepers of what was and wasn't beach music. Deejays would expand beach music's limits, and as a result a remarkable event took place in 1980.

Having watched a lot of dancers and bystanders, deejay Mike Lewis felt that some unconventional music might inject fresh energy into the scene. By and large, folks were dancing to the same old standards, some a bit worn in the grooves. Lewis, a deejay from Chapel Hill, played a song by Delbert McClinton at Fat Jack's Labor Day shag contest, and it paid dividends right away. McClinton's "A Mess o' Blues," with its easy tempo, sax, harmonica, and love-lorn lyrics, pulled people, even country music fans, to the dance floor. The song demonstrated the shag's adaptability, and thanks in part to McClinton, a spurt of countrified adrenalin gave the shag a boost. McClinton, no beach bum, grew up in music-prone Fort Worth. There his Texas roots blended with roadhouse rock, juke-joint blues, Memphis soul, and country, but with "Mess o' Blues" he had sung a beach song in a way.

Nashville writer Michael McCall described McClinton's tone as "a raspy, ferocious voice that carries in it the history of American popular music." That voice would carry a bit of shag history as well.

With the shag's renewal, old clubs that had provided venues for dancers during the dark ages became the new hot spots. Shag's embers erupted into flames. Parties lasting three days with shag contests pulled in thousands of ardent fans. Momentum built, and the dance again assumed regional allure. Dancers chartered buses to invitational parties such as Charleston's Geechee Blast and Rock Hill's Spring Fling. Frequent contest winners found a market eager for their expertise, and students desired to learn nimble footwork from these virtuosos. That 1950s cool was on the way back.

THE REUNION

Like the cheap lime-green leisure suits it spawned, the disco age proved short-lived. The Bee Gees, KC and the Sunshine Band, and Donna Summer faded away with disco, the baby boomers' last great popular dance.

As the shag traveled the long road back, as the revival built intensity, albums from beach music bands topped the charts. Along the beach people were spotting old familiar faces from the golden days when they worked together, but it was happenstance. There was no rhyme or reason to it. A sense of order and a predictable way to get together just didn't exist. Old beach bums of the glory days pined for those renowned times. Then an ex-lifeguard of the 1950s, a former beach bum, Gene Laughter (the name rhyming with "daughter"), came up with an idea that would make history. He just wanted to get the old gang together; shaggers were an afterthought. "There were not many back then," said Laughter, "just a handful of shaggers to begin with."

Like so many beach bums, Laughter had a nickname, "Swink," and he had something else: a penchant for playing practical jokes. He often tossed "SOS" bottles into the Atlantic to entertain his family on summer vacations.

In 1978 Swink put an SOS (Save Our Ship) note on aged parchment inside an antique bottle and pitched it into the Atlantic. The bottle, purporting to be from the *Ann Alexander,* washed ashore and ended up on the desk of *Charlotte Observer* reporters. The discovery received national media attention when the Charlotte Mint Museum deemed the note authentic and the wire services picked up the story.

It didn't take the Whaling Museum of New Bedford, Massachusetts, long to sniff out Laughter's ruse. The ship in question had sunk thirty years prior to the note's date. Since the hoax resulted in no money transactions, Laughter avoided legal troubles. Thanks to his hoax, though, journalists at the *Charlotte Observer,* Jerry Bledsoe and Kays Gary, became familiar with Laughter's name, connections that would prove useful.

In 1980 the glorious days of his youth were running through Laughter's mind. Perhaps memories of steering-wheel knobs and the smell of peroxide had taken him back in time. Something had. He had been quietly contacting a few friends about getting some of the old beach bums together. It wasn't easy tracking down friends, many known only by nicknames from bygone days, so he turned to Bledsoe to generate publicity for his reunion. Bledsoe's and Gary's features spread the word on the shag and the upcoming reunion, which still didn't seem to be a sure thing. A spark seemed necessary. How best to make a big splash?

The answer floated upon Atlantic breakers. People strolled the beaches looking for whatever gifts the sea might wash ashore. In 1980 the breakers pushed quite a surprise ashore. A passerby found an antique bottle, an A. O. Ashley Red Sea Balsam bottle, carrying a New Bedford, Massachusetts, imprint. Inside a note of distress on old parchment broadcast a plea:

> S.O.S. . . . . Reward for Delivery. Please see that this gets to Captain Earl Bostic of the U.S.S. Flamingo in the port of Charlestowne. Raven is rocking off the Carolina Banks. Migration is underway [*sic*]. Due at Oak Tree September 11th.
>
> James Ricks, Captain
> USS Raven
> 14 June 1897

Disaster had struck the USS *Raven*, a whaling vessel, eighty-three years earlier. All those years the bottle had wandered the seas without making landfall, a whale of a story. The *Sumter Daily Item* swallowed the bait this time and ran the story, which the Associated Press picked up.

The bottle at least was authentic; the message was not. Laughter had struck again. For a few days maritime experts gave the S.O.S. note their attention. In reality it was nothing more than a cryptic message extending an invitation to shaggers with enough savvy and inside info to decode the message. September 11—that was to be the day for the reunion at Ocean Drive. Bostic and Ricks were rhythm-and-blues leaders. "Flamingo" had been a hit record, and Oak Tree was a motel.

Laughter admitted that his latest bottle caper was yet another hoax. With a slip of paper and an old bottle Swink had kicked off his reunion with hope for a bit of media coverage. The word got out all right: "People can you hear it" . . . that old love for the beach is in the air. Pleased with his effort, Laughter anticipated that maybe five hundred people would attend the September 11, 1980, reunion, which fell on a Thursday.

As the brilliant fall weekend approached, people poured into O.D., known now, of course, as North Myrtle Beach. Laughter's astonishment grew. Word of mouth spread the message like wildfire. The old lifeguards, beach bums, dancers, waitresses—a litany of those who had been touched by the shag—came, and they kept coming.

The old habitués of Ocean Drive came by the droves, then by the hundreds. The migration seemed to have no end. Shaggers from the glory days flooded into Fat Jack's and the Afterdeck. The Oak Tree Inn sold out early. Gene had expected two to three hundred, but close to five thousand showed up. A reunion leading to a great revival was taking place.

CAPISTRANO FOR SHAGGERS

As people poured into O.D., the reunion began on a Wednesday. Gatherings and beer busts were held at Fat Jack's, the Oak Tree Inn, the Spanish Galleon, and other locations. The Friday beer bust at Fat Jack's made for quite a scene. As the crowd swelled, people compared hair colors and cracked jokes about receding hairlines. They resurrected those days when everyone had nicknames and everyone shagged.

"I was present at the very first S.O.S.," said Pat Tyler, "danced night and day all weekend surrounded by a crowd urging us on." Tyler's joy proved contagious. Many people danced the weekend away. What was to be a onetime party looked more like a tradition in the making. Gene Laughter knew a good thing when he saw it. He realized that the people, the music, the beach, and the reunion held tremendous potential. Years later (1988) he would tell a reporter for the *Greensboro News and Record* that the S.O.S. was "just an excuse for anyone who's forty-something to act like a kid again. I think we need our spring break just like the kids do."

Yes, Laughter knew what he was doing. He had hit upon a magical formula that would result in annual migrations. Shaggers, like swallows, need their own hallowed ground to return to year after year. His first beach-bum reunion was described as "an unmitigated, hip-swaying, elbow-bending, back-slapping success" in the September 13, 1980, *Sun News.*

Laughter would refer to his beach party for adults as a "state of mind, a fountain of youth." As the years rolled on, one woman would express what that formula did for her: "It's like a high school reunion without the nerds. It makes me feel youthful."

The lifeguards' hard muscles weren't so firm, and the lissome waitresses, well, Father Time had changed them too, but their hearts remained as young as ever. Two words described the reunion of these forever-young souls: unbridled joy. Everyone in attendance asked Laughter to make it an annual event. The title Society of Stranders (S.O.S.), a bit of a highbrow name, came to identify these migrating shaggers.

In September 1981 S.O.S. II took place, and in September 1982 S.O.S. III followed, the society all the while gaining strength. Former beach bums, life-guards, jitterbuggers, self-professed beach music freaks, and lovers of the Grand Strand converged on O.D. A report in the *State* newspaper described the reunion faithful as "an army of middleagers, graying, slightly paunchy returned to relive through conversation and dance the Grand Strand as they knew it back in the '40s and '50s."

That old theme of black music and whites intermingling continued to hold serve. Dodson wrote in 1982 that Ocean Drive boosted the careers of groups such as the Tams and the Drifters. He said, "In many cases, groups such as the Tams and Drifters got started by playing live before college crowds on Ocean Drive. In virtually every instance, the groups were black and the crowds were white and middle class, an irony in a region that was undergoing huge seismic shifts in race relations at the same time. The pairing, though odd, had solid justification . . . a lot of black performers found themselves excluded from popular radio play, not only in the South but all over the nation." Black groups' records, nonetheless, had ended up on jukeboxes, and young people loved what they heard during what for them would be an unforgettable time. Dodson said:

Entirely new audiences were introduced to the sound. Yet the prevail-ing beach music attitude around the clubs remained the same; it didn't particularly matter if the rest of the nation officially adopted the Caro-lina beach music culture. Its fans had been ignored for years. Even during periods when the music was at a low ebb in the South, clubs that played it survived in the style of speakeasy bars, attracting a crowd that was typically older but still clad in beach music mufti—the proverbial Bass Weejuns, khakis, and oxford-cloth shirts. For them, time stood still. No matter what the calendar year was outside, inside it was still an age when drinking beer and dancing the shag and making time with someone just met from a rival college meant something special. It was good guiltless fun, very material-istic, very middle-class. A line from a famous Tams song summed up the philosophy: Be young, be foolish, be happy.

COLD BEER AND WARM HEARTS

That old saying "The more things change, the more they remain the same" held currency for the old beach crowd. Dodson, who wrote his piece in 1982, quoted a onetime O.D. policeman and real estate man, serving up a prophecy in the process. Harold Bessent, he wrote, "sensed a new wave of beach music beginning to rise when a giant beach music festival drew a couple of thousand old-time enthusiasts like himself back to town for three weeks of shag dancing, beer drinking, and reminiscing about former glory days at the beach. 'The funny thing,' Bessent adds, 'is that an awful lot of younger people came in with the old crowd. Beach music has crossed the lines between three generations now. It's coming back stronger than ever.'"

Was it ever. Drinking cold beer, dancing, and having your heartstrings pulled proved to be as strong a combination as ever.

Swink Laughter's hoax would become a long-running hit. Besides dancing, associated events such as pool parties, fish fries, and other parties of all descriptions joined the festivities. Shaggers and Stranders came back to Ocean Drive in the spring and fall by the tens of thousands.

Fat Harold's, Duck's, Crazy Zack's, Harold's Across the Street, and the Galleon became shrines for devout Stranders who made the pilgrimages. Among those pilgrims was one Mike Marr.

Marr, former president of the York Shag Club and onetime S.O.S. *Carefree Times* editor, well remembers S.O.S. 2005. Marr and his wife, Diane, got back into the shag in the mid-1990s when they joined the York Shag Club. They attended their first S.O.S. in 1995 and have gone every year since. Marr wrote a colorful account about Swink Laughter on the occasion of the Spring Migration in 2005. "Jo Jo and the Parade" begins with a reference to *Butch Cassidy and the Sundance Kid* and the "Spring Safari" parade:

> Even though Butch and Sundance had run day and night and crossed several states, they weren't too concerned until they saw the hat. It was a white skimmer and that could only mean one person, Joe LaFores, the best lawman in the country.
>
> As we made the last turn in the Spring Safari parade we saw the hat, but this time it was a black fedora with the brim turned up in the front. This hat, too, could only mean one person. Jo Jo Putnam, a living legend, was ambling down the street toward us.

I introduced myself and told him that the last time I saw him was in Lake Wylie with two very young women on his arms. That was fifteen years ago. He thought for a moment, looked at the York Shag Club symbol on my shirt, and finally said, "I remember that." He went on to say, "My old friend, One Lung, is from York, does he come around anymore?"

I told him that Charles came to every meeting, especially since we had awarded him a lifetime membership. Jo Jo went into deep thought again before saying, "Charles Blackwell was the first Jitterbug I ever saw. That was way back in 1949."

With a little math I figured that One Lung was only 19 years old at the time. My brain just could not grasp that image. Jo Jo eased over to the motorcycle policeman who was helping with the parade and thrust both hands at him in submission, "Seems like old times," he said.

The 25th anniversary of S.O.S. did seem like old times. There were characters that no one had seen in years. It opened as usual with introductions. Judy Vick, our ACSC chairman, started reading an article by Phil Sawyer about how it all got started. It had something to do with a fellow named Swink Laughter. She was having trouble with the lighting and stumbled over several words. Finally, Ron Whisenant, S.O.S. president, stepped up to the mike and said, "Why don't we let Swink tell it in his own words."

A very distinguished older gentleman emerged from the shadows to an uproar of applause. He introduced himself and admitted he was probably responsible for all of us being there. He told us how he and a friend had got to talking about the old days and decided that they should throw a party and invite all the old lifeguards and beach bums to come. The problem was that they only knew most of them by nicknames. Names like One Lung, Hoofer, and so on. Swink knew a newspaperman in Charlotte who might be able to help. So they enlisted Kays Gary to get the word out. Gary promised he would do all he could with one stipulation: it had to be an open party, not private. ("I caught a lot of heat for letting anyone in," said Laughter in 2011, "but it wasn't my fault.")

With the party planned and a way to get to everyone, they visited the Chamber of Commerce in Ocean Drive and were quickly told that it was a great day when they left back in the 1950s and that they were not wanted back. They got similar respect at all the local clubs. At the point of giving up they decided to have a drink at the Oak Tree Inn to drown their sorrows. As the two were discussing how things had gone wrong, a gentleman at the end of the bar interrupted them. He said that he could not help noticing Swink's friend's pants, which had Snoopy and the Sopwith Camel all over them. He told them that if he could have those pants he thought he might be able to help them. Since the men were about the same size an agreement was made and they headed to the bathroom to exchange pants.

The man was the owner of the Oak Tree Inn and the party was back underway [*sic*]. They did not know whether to expect 30 people or 300, but they never expected the 5,000 that showed up for the very first S.O.S. way back in 1980.

The rest as they say is history, seems like old times.

LAUGHTER'S EPIC TALE recorded by Marr had a slight mistake and omitted some colorful details. Laughter himself wrote about that pivotal day of providence and flamboyant pants. He and Tom Lily were dog tired on that Saturday afternoon in the early summer of 1980. They had spent a long, fruitless day of hunting party space, a headquarters of sorts, for the first S.O.S. No luck at all. He and Lily were depressed as they stood at the Alpine Deli bar up in the Surfwood Shopping Center. They had been put down all day. The beach community wanted golfers, not old jitterbuggers, and as Laughter wrote, "Let's face it. We had zero credibility."

Lily stood out with his flashy pants. White and embellished with embroidered red and blue Snoopies piloting open-cockpit airplanes, the gaudy trousers embarrassed Laughter. "Snoopy was diving and flying all over Lily's pants," he observed. Lily and Laughter finished their first beer and ordered another round. Their mood changed. They laughed and joked around. Forget S.O.S. and its problems.

And then another one of those moments in the shag's colorful history transpired. A stranger walked up.

"I really like those pants," he said.

"You and I are about the same size," Lily replied, "You can have them. My friend here makes fun of them. We'll exchange pants." Lily and the stranger swapped pants in the men's room. Back at the bar the stranger admitted that he was fond of anything aeronautical since he owned an airplane. The fellow asked Laughter and Lily if they were golfers.

"No, we're here trying to plan a party for a bunch of old beach bums," explained Laughter. He went on to explain the great difficulty they were having finding a location for the as-yet-unborn S.O.S.

"Come with me," the stranger replied. "I own a large oceanfront hotel. It's on its knees, about belly up . . . and it's yours. Use it as you wish! Let's go down to my hotel right now for drinks and dinner!"

The stranger's name was Gordon McLean. His hotel was the Oak Tree Inn, made notorious in Laughter's S.O.S. bottle hoax. That inn most likely saved the S.O.S. from being just another great idea. The Oak Tree Inn soon became the Maritime Beach club, and it served the S.O.S. for its first three migrations before a time-sharing concept made it inaccessible.

The migrations continued, and the 2005 reunion was just like old times, as Marr wrote. Ocean Drive had become North Myrtle Beach, but one thing had not died: the blazing memories of misspent youth. Shaggers crammed into O.D., and hotels sold out. To the old guard, Ocean Drive was sacrosanct—and there, like the legendary phoenix, the shag rose from the ashes of disco and the British Invasion, and this time it would not fade away. Few groups have institutionalized their youth as the S.O.S. has.

Yearning is one powerful affliction. Its most obvious symptom is a wistful affection for the past. In 1944, just about the time the shag was to take off, Doris Day sang "Sentimental Journey," a song of nostalgia. That song could well have been written for Swink Laughter. He had long lamented the loss of the, for want of a better word, primitive days of the early 1950s. Some three decades after recapturing the dream, Laughter would reminisce in *Carefree Times* about the old days:

> Was talking with "Bird" Keistler the other day, and as usual, the subject of the halcyon, golden years came up. "Bird" reminded me how primitive things were at O.D. in the early '50s. It's really hard to conceive now.
>
> No air conditioning. I mean none! Except at a couple of restaurants like Zane's and maybe Hoskin's. . . . Yet we wore our tailored wool flannel pants, long sleeve basket-weave shirts, and cashmere sweaters all summer long. What happened to those brisk cool night breezes from the sea? Maybe the high-rise condos and plastic, chrome and glitter have screened them off? Oh, we had a few hot, still nights when we had to go out on the beach and sleep on a float, but normally we were very comfortable clad in our summer woolens.
>
> There was only one telephone that we could use on the beach as we recall and that was at McElveen's Drug Store. And once you went past the Douglas McArthur Hotel there was a narrow two-lane dirt road to Cherry Grove Beach. In fact, there wasn't much asphalt paving at O.D. Just Main Street from Highway 17 to the stoplight at Ocean Boulevard and from the Douglas McArthur south to the light at Crescent.
>
> Almost none of the guys at the beach had cars. Wheels were a rarity, indeed! There were a few fat cats with cars. . . . Thumbing, or hitch hiking,

was the only way to go. We went everywhere by thumb. Down to Spivey's. To Charlotte. To Columbia.

Yea, those were the days.

Fun indeed. Shaggers were the original party animals. The party that began in the late 1940s hadn't ended. It had just taken a break, a hiatus that would see the emergence of landlocked shag clubs across the Carolinas. Here and there in unpretentious southern cities shaggers would meet, establish friendships, and reminisce about the legendary days at O.D. The stage was being set for a cultlike organization that would grow and migrate three times a year to North Myrtle Beach.

Still, a lot had to happen for shag's next golden age to unfold. Some shaggers had yet to hear what Laughter's hoax had pulled off. One thing was clear, though: the southern Atlantic Seaboard would never be the same now that the fabled fountain of youth had at last been discovered, thanks in part to a crazy pair of pants and a note in a bottle.

8

The Big Fusion

Despite many shaggers' dislike for the Beatles, "Come Together" proved apropos considering that the Fab Four disbanded on December 31, 1970. Ten years after the front men of the British Invasion split, the 1980s ushered in an era that would bring growth to the Society of Stranders and something else: strife.

Shaggers came together in the 1980s, but then their unity fractured. As things unraveled, the Beatles' ironic song amounted to a plea. Could shaggers come together? Could they conquer the dissension and hard feelings that promised to stop their resurgence in its shoes?

THE 1980S WERE GOOD YEARS in more ways than one. Shag clubs kept forming and growing, driven by the dreams and memories of the dance's disciples. Older and wiser, shag's devotees displayed their love for their smooth dance with level heads often missing in their youth. They had grown up. And so had the shag. No longer was it a "dirty dance" done to "dirty music."

In shaggers' rearview mirrors lay the days of lying about their whereabouts, fistfights at White Lake's Crystal Club and O.D., and the ritual of being locked up by O.D. police chief Merlin "the Wizard," Bellamy. Said the Wizard, "I only did what I was told to do." The S.O.S. would give Bellamy a place in the Hall of Fame in time.

Shaggers were recapturing their youth albeit in a more responsible manner. Once at odds with Ocean Drive's powers, the shaggers and their money were now welcome in O.D., a decided departure from the old days. Still, trouble was brewing. Call it growing pains. How best to move forward as a more cohesive dance society?

Back in 1980 Swink Laughter had given the beach bums who reconnected at that first reunion a name, the Society of Stranders, a not-so-subtle tribute to the Grand Strand. That society has its own story to tell.

Throughout the mid- to late 1980s, the S.O.S. would grow in strength. Shaggers and Stranders came back to Ocean Drive in the spring and fall by the thousands. Their story attracted a lot of attention.

Smithsonian magazine covered the beach music–shag phenomenon some twenty years after Swink Laughter's legendary S.O.S. bottle caper. The September 2000 issue published a feature, "The Jitterbug Met R&B," by T. Edward Nickens, who wasted no time describing shag's holy ground: "With my back to a hot pink souvenir shop hawking body piercing, Free Hermit Crabs, and 59-cent saltwater taffy, I'd have no trouble bouncing a rock off the doors of a half-dozen beach music clubs. Ducks and Ducks Too, OD Café, OD Arcade and Lounge, and Pirates Cove would be a cinch. Fat Harold's—now Fat Harold's would take some doing. Maybe two stones' throws, tops."

Nickens's rocks, unlike those of the hippie protestors, were just a figure of speech, and yet during this crucial period when shaggers were forming organizations, hostilities surfaced. No shaggers threw rocks at each other, but challenges existed—nothing new. Shaggers had already endured trials such as the dark ages, as Nickens pointed out in *Smithsonian*:

> From the beach the shag migrated inland and found fertile ground in country club and cotton crossroads alike. For years the shag was a fixture of Southern culture. You shagged at sock hops, debutante parties, fraternity dances. You shagged in abandoned parking lots and at the end of dead-end roads. And during the summers, you made a pilgrimage to the ramshackle bars and jukebox dives that dotted the Southern shore.
>
> For a few dark decades, the shag was pushed into the margins of Southern life. Elvis and the Beatles put a new twist on the dance floor, and in 1954 Hurricane Hazel turned much of the shagging coast to rubble.

WAS IT ALL A DREAM?

From the rubble of Hazel and more, the shag had risen. Nickens summed up the shag's comeback, though he omitted Swink Laughter's legendary bottle caper: "Then, in 1980, an ex-lifeguard named Gene Laughter planned a reunion of beach bums at O.D. . . . The notion of a formal shagging organization was planted, and the shag renaissance commenced."

The revival began minus much of its youthful energy because an unavoidable change called adulthood had put the shag on a back burner, a cold burner at that. "After a time, too, the architects of shag were, well, architects," wrote Nickens. "And bosses and employees, mamas, and daddies. The dance was still a staple of country club weekends, but shagging as a central focus of life was history."

The responsibilities of life, career, and parenting caught up with the children of O.D. even as cultural changes derailed their dream. Their youth paled, peroxided, you could say, by Father Time. Still, thanks in part to the Laughter-inspired revival, shaggers would get their mojo back in the 1980s. Shag clubs and shag nightclubs would spring up, giving people a place to shag the night away when the beach was not just out of reach but still out of vogue too due to lingering effects of the dark ages.

In 1984 a song hit the air. Though no shag song, Don Henley's "The Boys of Summer" expressed shaggers' lonesome plight. The song grieves for empty beaches and the loss of a dream. Fabled summers seem to be but a memory. Henley's song appears to be a lament about the passing of youth, with a dash of summer love thrown in for good measure. A shag song it's not, but its lyrics and haunting melody hint of the love, mystery, and power those magical days at O.D. wielded. Now that shaggers had recaptured a bit of that magic, how best to get it going again?

Shaggers faced two choices: get together in ad hoc fashion or bring unity, purpose, and permanence to their resurgence.

IT WAS A WEDNESDAY NIGHT in 1979 in Columbia, South Carolina. At a newly minted beach club called Wit's End, Phil and Chick Sawyer met Sherry and Nick Mathis. The music was hard-core beach. As people met, the clink of long-neck brown bottles punctuated the music. Local shaggers got to know each other. Word got around, and the group grew.

September 1980. Wit's End shaggers went to Ocean Drive for something called the S.O.S.—an event they knew little about. It was shrouded in mystery. After a weekend of dancing, their world would never be the same again.

The group returned to Columbia and danced winter nights away at Wit's End with an occasional foray "across the river" to Fanny Teague's, another new beach club a stone's throw from Irmo, South Carolina.

The seeds of organization kept sprouting. Clubs sprang up all over Columbia, and not just Columbia. Beach music played in the clubs and on the radio. The big question of the day was, "where y'all going tonight?" The answer was, "Across the river to start, but we'll be back on this side by midnight."

Therein lay a problem. As more and more shag dance clubs arose, close-knit groups began to scatter. Dancers went here; dancers went there. With more and more beach clubs forming, party nights were watered down, weak beer. The time to organize had arrived.

The Wit's End shaggers mobilized, forming the Columbia Shag Club in 1982. It had one goal: to enhance the enjoyment of shagging and introduce it to others. Nick Mathis would be its first president.

At the same time clubs were sprouting up, the S.O.S. was growing. So was development in and around O.D. Motels were transformed into condominiums and time-sharing facilities. First-class accommodations became scarce, and for a brief time talk centered on moving S.O.S. to Surfside. Shaggers' love for O.D. prevailed, and O.D. remained the heartland for all things shag. Development was planting the seeds for a collision, however.

Clubs kept mushrooming. Beach music clubs in the inland cities of North and South Carolina began to bring back the rhythm-and-blues tunes of shaggers' youth, along with some good new music. Shagging was off and dancing, you could say.

The Columbia Shag Club had organized about six months before the Rock Hill Area Shag Club became South Carolina's second club. In Charlotte, North Carolina, a hotbed for the shag, students of the shag trailblazer Shad Alberty would organize as the Metrolina Shag Club.

Nearby in Rock Hill, Ron Whisenant was turning over an idea. Why not form a shag association? Whisenant and Sawyer, by now the Columbia Shag Club's second president, met in the winter of 1983 to discuss just that—forming an association from five South Carolina shag clubs that had been partying together on Sunday afternoons.

Whisenant and Sawyer met several times to formulate the concept and develop a charter. They didn't want the association to be a tyrant commanding local clubs to do this and that, so they established a board of advisers in lieu of a board of directors.

In addition they handled an important matter with aplomb. The association would not be "work-oriented." There would be no awards for increasing membership and raising money. It would, in the spirit of the shag, be a good-time organization only. The agenda had one item: partying.

THE ASSOCIATION IS FORMED

Club representatives met in February 1984 in Columbia to establish the nonprofit Association of Carolina Shag Clubs (ACSC). "Carolina" referred to the dance, not a geographical area. Charter members came from Charleston, Columbia, Rock Hill, Greenville, Winnsboro, and the Atlanta Shag Club. Ron Whisenant of Rock Hill served as the association's first president.

Local clubs continued to sponsor statewide parties. Soon Columbia, Charleston, Atlanta, Greenville, Rock Hill, and Winnsboro were hosting regular weeklong events, which other clubs attended. Structure and purpose had arrived.

The fledgling association's first foray was a cruise. More than 150 shaggers boarded the SS *Galileo* on March 3, 1984, for a five-day Caribbean holiday, the first of many cruises to destinations such as South America, the Grand Caymans, the Virgin Islands, Mexico, and the California coast, as well as a never-to-be-forgotten weeklong fantasy on Waikiki Beach in Honolulu.

Fabulous trips became the ACSC's forte, and the association's success spread. Ken Hudspeth followed Whisenant as chairman, and the Metrolina became the first North Carolina club to become a member. All the while S.O.S. contests, invitational weekends, and events at the beach began to flourish. The second mid-winter shag meet (it had no name) took place in January 1985 at Fat Harold's in Ocean Drive, aka North Myrtle Beach.

The clubs and statewide parties prospered. Another cruise took place. Meanwhile Laughter's S.O.S. was becoming bigger and bigger even as cities all over North and South Carolina, Florida, Georgia, and Virginia were forming clubs. A club's first order of business was to join the association. The S.O.S. and the ACSC were headed for an encounter that would shake the shag world.

In 1986 the Shaggers Hall of Fame inducted the association as a member. In 1987 Phil Sawyer assumed association leadership, which he would hold for three years. By now the association consisted of eighteen clubs.

The association took on more structure and requirements. Growth necessitated a bit more businesslike approach. Any club joining the association had to have a charter, bylaws, elected officials, membership dues, a newsletter, regular meetings, and attendance at association workshops. Association membership increased from eighteen to forty-five clubs.

Other associations came into being. The Shaggers Preservation Association was formed in November 1981 to oversee shag contests, and the Association of Beach and Shag Club DeeJays arose for those spinning the records so dear to shaggers. The two major organizations were growing side by side: Laughter's Society of Stranders and the Association of Carolina Shag Clubs.

Like birds migrating to the shores of their genesis, dance-smitten people had been returning to the beach of their youth's passions as predictably as the tides. For a long time their migration had been spontaneous, but the Society of Stranders was giving it structure and purpose. Shaggers now flocked to Ocean Drive like swallows to Capistrano.

S.O.S. EVOLVES

As shag clubs proliferated, the S.O.S. forged on, but its future was no lock. Its party format changed. At first there were contests and bands. Many dance clubs levied cover charges. Clubs opened and closed, changing hands from one season to the next. The S.O.S. encountered logistical problems in securing places to hold organization parties. Club continuity was a *rara avis,* and getting consistent deals didn't happen.

Neither were all those youthful years of bad behavior forgotten; a hangover of drunken revelry persisted. The North Myrtle Beach city fathers didn't quite know what to do with the Society of Stranders—encourage or prevent, support or squash. No one quite knew what to make of it, at least not yet. But a few did. In the early 1980s North Myrtle Beach mayor Joe Saleeby remarked of the S.O.S., "It's the best thing to hit the Grand Strand since the jukebox was invented."

Despite the uncertainty, Laughter realized more than anyone else the potential of his new product. The unbridled joy of everyone who attended sent a loud, clear message: "This is too good to be true. Keep it going and even expand."

S.O.S. II and S.O.S. III had brought a member database, publications, and organized events. Membership cards replaced cover charges for entrance to the clubs. The Boogie Boat, a shagger's ferry, proved unworkable. Contests and bands were eliminated. Deejays took over.

One thing didn't change. Shaggers came back to Ocean Drive in the spring and fall by the thousands for what everyone agreed were the country's finest parties, now referred to as "Spring" and "Fall Migrations." Everyone who ever had one grain of sand in his shoes agreed that to miss one was unthinkable. Beach clubs such as Fat Harold's, Duck's, Crazy Zack's, Harold's Across the Street, and the Galleon became shrines to which devout Stranders pilgrimaged several times each year.

Meanwhile, Laughter found life more demanding. Overseeing his growing shag organization amounted to a second full-time job. As well he served as editor of *Carefree Times,* the society's newsletter. In a special Fall Migration issue of *Carefree Times,* Laughter lifted the veil on some serious family matters.

The year 1986 proved to be a disastrous one for the Laughter family. Black clouds hung over them for six months. His son-in-law, Phil Summers, died in his sleep on February 6 at the age of thirty-two. Summers was Laughter's right arm when it came to running the S.O.S. In May, Laughter's wife, Nadine, received a diagnosis of breast cancer. In mid-July Laughter's daughter was rushed to the hospital with a rupture that resulted from an ectopic pregnancy. After an emergency operation, a cascading series of complications ensued, and she ended up in intensive care for two weeks. Laughter described it as "an absolute nightmare."

During these family tragedies and crises Laughter did his best to plan the fall S.O.S. Migration and put together the S.O.S. yearbook, a monstrous undertaking. The pressure built. His wife begged him to give up the S.O.S.

Wrote Laughter, "S.O.S. has become an albatross with an insatiable appetite that literally gobbles up huge chunks of my fleeting spare time. In tough times like these working on S.O.S. just may be one of the few things that has allowed me to maintain even a *thin thread of sanity.* And there remains a final personal challenge. I would like to see the S.O.S. through its 10th anniversary in 1990. After that, who knows?"

An outpouring of notes, calls, and prayers came Laughter's way, and then 1987 came and went. The early summer 1988 newsletter edition hints of the demands the S.O.S. was making on Laughter. In the lower right-hand corner of page 3 he described himself as "Publisher, Editor, Columnist, Advertising Hack, Complaint Manager, Mail Room Boy, Janitor, Chief Go-fer, Etc."

"Complaint Manager" sticks out like a sore thumb. There comes a time when too much is too much. Laughter had founded, owned, and operated the S.O.S. since its beginning in 1979. Under his leadership the event had grown to two revered weekend parties a year with five to six thousand attending. Laughter, however, had health and work-related problems that made running the S.O.S. burdensome.

FAT HAROLD'S BEACH CLUB

Through the jukebox doors you'll find shag memorabilia, photos from
the old days, and a board from the Pad in this beach club museum.

*Photograph by Robert Clark. Courtesy of Harvey and
Selene Graham, owners, 94.9 "The Surf" radio.*

CLASSIC ROCK-OLA

David Cullen Rockola founded the Rock-Ola Corporation in 1927 some two decades before rock rocked the land. Some believe that Rock-Ola inspired the term "rock and roll." For sure it spread that evil "race music."

Photograph by Robert Clark.

45 RPM

What joy round vinyl brought. Popular music's dominant format
from 1955 for decades on gave us the terms "single," "one-hit wonder,"
"A-side," "B-side," and "payola." Jukeboxes could change 45s faster:
no need to wait for that Swingin' Medallion song.

Photograph by Robert Clark.

ICONIC DOORKNOB

The most utilitarian of doorknobs taught many a beginner the basic step. Just loop a string around the doorknob, practice the steps, muster up the courage, and head for O.D.

Photograph by Robert Clark.

SPRING SAFARI PARADE

Wacky, zany—these words describe the last Saturday of the Spring S.O.S. parade down North Myrtle Beach's Main Street. Even Elvis, onetime shag adversary, made an appearance on floats vying for awards in four categories.

Photograph by Tom Poland.

DEEJAY

Many people consider deejays keepers of what is and what isn't beach music. Said Jimmy Buffkin, "Taking requests from the crowd is very important and if I've got it, I'll play it. If I am playing for a crowd of three hundred, or a crowd of 10, having the dance floor full is my goal!"

Photograph by Robert Clark.

DANCING TO THE BEAT

Vanessa and Bryant Stephens, members of the Carolina Shag Club, got
interested in the shag in 2003. Shag music for them can be most any genre. It
has to have just one requirement: that shag beat that gets them up and moving.

Photograph by Robert Clark.

MISSISSIPPI BLUES TRAIL MARKER

Blues aficionados consider legendary Robert Johnson's twenty-nine recordings from 1936 to 1937 to mark an artistic high point of the blues. Johnson died in Greenwood, Mississippi, on August 16, 1938.

Photograph by Wanda Harper Clark, courtesy of Jim O'Neal, BluEsoterica Archives, and Mississippi Blues Trail

THREADS OF MEMORIES

For years Ellen Taylor collected shag club and special-event T-shirts. She donated them to become a quilt that will take its place in a future shag museum. Beverly Cone, quilter, designed and made the quilt, a piece of one-of-a-kind memorabilia that preserves the memories of South Carolina's state dance.

Photograph by Robert Clark.

Organizational headaches were surfacing as well. The day was approaching when he would have to decide between his career and the movement he helped create. Even the official 1987 S.O.S. Spring Safari bumper sticker, "Shag Naked," brought Laughter grief. Of the slogan Laughter had said, "It's about time we focus on the fact that not only college kids have fun. They have their spring break. Now we have ours. If the kids can have 'Party Naked' and 'Surf Naked' bumper stickers and T-shirts, then we'll go one up on them."

Laughter's reward? Accusations of pornography. Laughter defended his slogan as cute, not a dare. Still, criticism poured in, and the slogan died. Off-color bumper stickers and T-shirts were small potatoes compared to what was coming. The last thing Laughter needed was strife of a serious kind. Laughter once quipped, "Go for the jugular of life." Now life was going for his jugular. Divisive days were ahead.

TROUBLE BREWS

In that same early summer 1988 *Carefree Times,* Laughter wrote a revealing column, "SOSers, Stand Up & Be Counted." Its title could have been "Come Together, Right Now."

Good intentions started the trouble. During the fall 1987 and spring 1988 S.O.S. parties, a group of Stranders held an invitation-only party at the Spanish Galleon, one of the stalwart dance clubs. This event ran against the shag nation's code of togetherness and generated discord among the beach club owners—a threat to the annual parties themselves. If you have no place to dance, you have a big problem.

The group behind the party adopted the unwieldy name the Tradition and Preservation of Shaggers Society, T.A.P.S. Leading the organization was Mit Starbuck, a man of ambition who fired off many a letter in all caps. His exclusive party amounted to a revolt. To quell the uprising, Laughter shot straight with the shag nation: "Any large group of people will eventually have splits, splinters, and spin-offs. Political organizations. Even churches. It's inevitable. It's human nature. S.O.S. has had it's [*sic*] share of splinter groups. They come . . . and they go. None, so far, have had the tenacity to last. Building a viable, lasting beach party organization is a slow one-step-at-a-time process. Believe me, I know."

Strife and confusion set in. In 1988 the Spanish Galleon denied T.A.P.S. the use of its facilities for the "Grand Party." Wrote Starbuck in irritating all caps, as was his style, "It appears the Spanish Galleon has chosen to join in on the 'mammonistic' [*sic*] traditions that S.O.S. seems to have created over the years." He then proceeded to list complaints about S.O.S. and accused it of taking advantage of the good ol' folks who had supported the beach since the 1940s.

Starbuck then spent the rest of his newsletter apologizing to readers who had taken offense at perceived insults and intimidation. Communication, to be blunt, was not his forte. The petty shag wars continued, and other letters indicative of bad blood went back and forth.

In 1989 T.A.P.S. sponsored a "Fall Shag Ball" from September 14 to the 17th at Crazy Zack's in O.D. Starbuck sent a flyer out that made an emphatic point of stressing that S.O.S. cards would not be honored and that members of T.A.P.S. would be admitted free.

Starbuck put out another divisive flyer in 1989 with a special notation: "We at T.A.P.S. are more interested in organizing a 'shag oriented' membership that is void of rednecks, derelicts, drug addicts, and non-shaggers than we are in money or profit."

T.A.P.S. let serious bad blood set in, influencing Harold Worley, who owned the Spanish Galleon and the O.D. Motel. He purchased Fat Harold's property, which gave him power over the location of Fat Harold's—operated by Harold Bessent, a staunch confederate to the S.O.S. Moreover Worley advised Laughter that a group of "five influential North Myrtle Beach shaggers" had approached him to form their own organization to compete with the S.O.S. Worley notified Laughter that the Galleon would not be available to S.O.S. members during the Fall Migration and that it would be available only to members of the competing organization.

Laughter's column addressed the threat to overthrow much of what he had built:

> Many of you will be receiving (or have received) a letter soliciting memberships in this new organization. I'm sure their list of membership advantages will be long and their dues will be much less than S.O.S. Worley will pump the big bucks into the T.A.P.S. endeavor for they need to make a big impact very quickly.
>
> Mr. Worley did give S.O.S. first refusal of using the Galleon, provided that I *give up control of S.O.S. by making him a partner and leave Harold Bessent.*

Worley was attempting a coup d'état predicated on big plans. If successful in evicting Fat Harold's, Worley planned to tear down the old building to build an ultramodern mega-complex with high-rise motel and enlarged club facilities. "S.O.S.," wrote Laughter, "would then have a permanent home. No more musical clubs."

Laughter continued, driving home a message anchored in one value alone: loyalty. He wrote,

> Shouldn't we go with Mr. Worley? He has a proven track record of fantastic financial success. He says he would bring a lot to the S.O.S. table. Play it safe and go with Mr. Worley, the man with the plan? Right?
>
> Wrong! You roll the dice! You maintain your freedom! You keep the options open.

Laughter's passion for what he had started burned through his rebuke. His words zipped out in staccato fashion, and he hit the nail on the head as to what was at stake. He wrote, "And you stand by an old friend who has been loyal to the S.O.S. for years! The big question is: *Will Harold Bessent be operating in his old location come this September?* Mr. Worley makes a case that Harold will be out."

FAT HAROLD

Wearing now-retro-looking glasses, former Ocean Drive policeman Harold Bessent has long been an ally to the S.O.S. Bessent and the S.O.S. created much of today's shag scene.

Photograph courtesy of Becky Stowe.

Laughter's words were prophetic. In the years to come, Harold Bessent would be a friend to all things shag, though in time he too would express his unhappiness with S.O.S.

"We'll stick with the fat one," said Laughter; "we'll sink or swim with the man who has done more for shaggers and beach music over the years than *anyone* at Ocean Drive Beach. He stuck by us . . . and with beach music, through thick and thin. And believe me, like S.O.S., Harold Bessent has seen his lean years and payed [sic] his dues."

Laughter went on to drive home the point that Bessent had done much to help the S.O.S. when it was struggling and losing money. Throughout the years and repeated in S.O.S. publications was a constant theme: how vital Harold Bessent had been to shaggers' cause. Many times it was pointed out the S.O.S. wouldn't be what it was without Bessent's support. Laughter's words conveyed the do-or-die role Bessent played in the survival of the S.O.S. He said:

> Were it not for my friendship with Harold Bessent, I would have folded the tent after S.O.S. III for I was ready to throw in the towel. Harold encouraged me to keep it going—for just one more year.
>
> S.O.S. and Harold Bessent worked in tandem to develop much of today's adult beach party shagging scene. We didn't swoop in to skim off the cream but labored long and hard together to make it a reality.

WACKY, KOOKY, CREATIVE

Laughter devoted a whole page to his editorial. His passion came through loud and clear. And so did a hint of anger. All that he had put together was under attack. He wrote:

> It's damn ironic, and wryly amusing, that T.A.P.S. plans to hold their beach party on the *same weekend as S.O.S.* Don't they have the creativity (and the guts) to pull it off on their own? Must they piggyback on the ability of S.O.S. to draw a crowd?
>
> If Mr. Worley really has the confidence that his organization will be such a success, then why doesn't he pick *another weekend* for *his* party and take advantage of *two crowds* at the Galleon and the O.D. Motel—both the S.O.S. and T.A.P.S. weekends?

Laughter's editorial scored point after point, even going as far as to remind the Stranders what they were all about from day one. He wrote: "The S.O.S.

philosophy is in direct contrast to the cool businesslike approach of Mr. Worley. S.O.S. started as a lark. It's a fun organization. It was never intended to be a business. S.O.S. just evolved. There was no plan. The business aspect took a back seat. The fun had to come first. The priorities were, and are, completely backwards and defy logic. S.O.S. is a wacky, kooky, creative operation. *A hard-nosed businessman could not have pulled it off!* Only a compulsive eccentric could have made S.O.S. work (and that just happened to be me)."

Laughter had planned to walk away from his society in 1990, after its tenth anniversary. "Perhaps this new challenge will provide the stimuli . . . the impetus . . . and the renewed energy to carry on," he wrote. "If the S.O.S. is not providing you with the fun and breaks from your work-a-day world . . . and at a price that you're completely comfortable with, *then I should walk away . . . and now!* If you don't care if the S.O.S. becomes fractured and fades away, then join T.A.P.S. and march (and shag) to the beat of a different drummer . . . at the Galleon," he wrote.

Over the years hundreds of shaggers, grateful for what Laughter had done, had asked him what they could do to help him. Laughter hurled his gauntlet down at the shag nation's feet. Closing his thirteen-hundred-word decree rife with italics for emphasis, Laughter turned to them: "I'm calling in your markers. Here's your chance! If you want S.O.S. to continue, then you can help by sticking with us and with Fat Harold. Support only the S.O.S. participating clubs at this S.O.S. Fall Migration. Show solidarity! Cast your lot with S.O.S. and Harold Bessent . . . stick with 'the ones that "brung you" to the dance.' The future of the S.O.S. is in your hands . . . and shaggin' feet. And that future, my friends, is *NOW!* The choice is yours."

PETTY SHAG WARS OF 1989

Laughter showed a sense of fair play; he gave his challengers free press. In the mid-summer 1988 issue of *Carefree Times,* he ran a notice on the front page, an update. T.A.P.S. had changed its name to Shagtime. Wrote Laughter, "The new organization being formed by Ed Moore and 'Cotton' Worley, which will hold beach parties at the Galleon competing with the S.O.S., which we referred to in the last issue of *Carefree Times,* is now being called Shagtime."

Laughter then ran another editorial, "S.O.S.—It's the Real Thing." He related how the S.O.S. had received a lukewarm reception in its early years and how people were now trying to exploit a good thing. He wrote, "The North Myrtle business community in general, and the beach clubs in particular, showed little interest in the S.O.S. during those early years. Only Harold

Bessent really dug in and helped. . . . Slowly, one step at a time, the organization grew, and then, all of a sudden, it exploded and became a financial success. Now everyone's interested."

Laughter seemed beleaguered and a bit angry. He said, "Now one of the newcomer clubs wants the lion's share—not satisfied with a slice of the pie, they want the whole thing. The petty shag wars have started and now ego, jealousy, and greed have reared their ugly heads."

Laughter felt he was the victim of the classic squeeze play. The new players were trying to force Laughter, the S.O.S., and Bessent out. Worley made good on his threat by serving eviction papers on Bessent. The Johnny-come-latelies wreaked havoc with contractual agreements and commitments. Not only did they hurt S.O.S.'s ability to conduct business, but they also tossed personal attacks, rumors, distortions, and innuendo into the fray. Shagtime, it should be noted, was less decorous than S.O.S., sponsoring events such as a wet T-shirt contest. Then disputes arose over which clubs S.O.S. members were welcome at during the fall 1988 party.

S.O.S. membership cards also caused a ruckus. The twenty-dollar card membership per year for S.O.S. members would prove especially controversial during the summer of 1989. To get into S.O.S. events at clubs, members supposedly had to show their cards, but some clubs didn't check for cards, making the card fee appear a rip-off. Shagtime ridiculed the membership fee as being way overpriced. Letters from S.O.S. members expressed outrage.

One read, "Dear Gene and S.O.S., We think you are a money hungry con man. You need to be sued for false representation and fraud, including mail fraud. . . . You took $20 from everyone at S.O.S. and gave them nothing in return." The writers, a married couple, went on to demand refund of all money taken in since 1980 or Laughter and S.O.S. would "find yourselves in the hands of the law." They demanded their money back ($360) or Laughter could expect to hear from their lawyers.

One woman wrote saying she was never asked to show her card. "I would like to ask for my $20 to be returned," she requested.

Then Bessent entered the fray. He wrote a letter disassociating himself and his clubs from the S.O.S. Bessent's unhappiness stemmed from his belief that one Mit Starbuck had taken over the S.O.S. from Laughter. All of this turbulence was 180 degrees opposite Laughter's intentions.

Laughter had created a vehicle for uniting old friends, and he took pride in bringing happiness to so many and was not about to stand by and watch infighting destroy the S.O.S. He had left the beach with tears in his eyes on the occasion of the first S.O.S. Migration in 1980. He had struggled to get the organization off the ground and had dug deep into his own pockets to keep things rolling. He had hand-addressed every newsletter and envelope he mailed out. He had paid his dues, but the weight of running S.O.S. had become too much.

Laughter responded yet again to all the controversy and accusations: "Shagtime says that S.O.S. members are being 'ripped-off' at $20 dues per year. This is an insult to S.O.S.ers. We aren't exactly stupid!"

Laughter chided the upstarts for riding the coattails of S.O.S. and pointed out that "the whole shagging and beach party scene grew to what it is today without these guys." The S.O.S., with its dues, said Laughter, "is the real deal."

Laughter handled it all. True, he had the help of a lot of people, and some, as Harry Driver pointed out, "did not feel he handled it the way they would have. This may be true, but handle it he did." Some Stranders didn't like the idea that Laughter was making a lot of money off them. Some said he was "getting wealthy."

Back in the mid-summer 1987 issue of *Carefree Times,* Laughter had advertised his four-bedroom condo for sale, saying, "They just aren't making any more ocean front lots!" That perhaps didn't help his cause among those resentful of him.

The time of the 1988 S.O.S. Fall Migration came. It was the Migration of the "shag wars," as Laughter referred to it, "pitting a parasitic come-lately group against our old traditional standby organization." The hostilities commenced.

Worley evicted Bessent from the Fat Harold's building due to a minor technicality in the lease. An eviction hearing had been scheduled for September 6, but the hearing was continued to September 22, making it possible for the S.O.S. revelry to spill over into Fat Harold's. Then Don "Pancake" Kelley, who held the lease, waffled and assigned the lease to Worley. Bessent was ordered out on Saturday, September 17, at 5:00 P.M., but he refused to leave until after S.O.S. had its "Last Hurrah" at Fat Harold's on Sunday, September 18. Shaggers showed up to show Bessent just how many S.O.S. friends he had.

Despite the bad blood, the crowd was bigger than ever. Beach music lovers came from twenty-seven states and three countries. Still, turmoil made things uncertain. S.O.S. membership renewals for 1989 were frozen.

Where would the S.O.S. go from here?

GRAY HAIR AND GREEN BANANAS

The summer of 1988 was long and difficult. Preparing for the Fall Migration while fighting the shag wars proved onerous. The road ahead, well, who knew where it would lead. Laughter speculated about the future in the program for the ninth Fall Migration: "As I have said many times before, we don't buy green bananas. The S.O.S. has faced adversity before and things always seem to work out, but at the last minute too often at the sake of my graying hair."

Back in 1987 on the occasion of the eighth fall party, an anonymous post in *Carefree Times* jokingly referred to the S.O.S. as a hydra-headed monster. The reality was that Laughter's beautiful creation was turning into Medusa—a serpent-coiffed monster. The future was uncertain. Would Harold Bessent open another club in O.D.? How many S.O.S. members would defect to the upstart organization? Would a Shagtime party simultaneous with the S.O.S. party tax the available beach club square footage?

Laughter sounded defiant. He wrote, "Of this much I'm damn sure: there will be an S.O.S. Spring Safari and an S.O.S. Fall Migration next year!!"

Laughter may have been confident, but the splinter group confused Stranders, as one letter to Laughter revealed. It read: "I hear there's a spin-off of the S.O.S. which plans to have a party for the old-timers next February. Will S.O.S. members be invited? What's the story?"

About this time a fortuitous event transpired in Columbia. Laughter came to know Phil Sawyer while letting a group sponsor a shag contest under S.O.S. auspices at the infamous Thunderbird Inn "up on the hill" in Columbia's St. Andrews district. Laughter encountered troubles with the mailing labels for S.O.S. I and II in 1981 and 1982. Sawyer told Laughter he'd take care of the list, a small act that would matter in a big way. Sawyer would become a close associate and consultant to Laughter. Their friendship would play a pivotal role in 1989 to the future of the S.O.S., for all was not well.

From 1988 to 1989 business interests at the beach fractured. Competition for dance room became fierce, and conflicts blazed. As one writer put it, "the holiest shrine in the entire shag world was irreverently destroyed." Meanwhile shaggers were calling Laughter constantly at his job. Then one day the receptionist accidentally routed a shagger's call to the company president. The president called Laughter in and gave him an ultimatum. Laughter—the S.O.S. mastermind, originator, and owner—was faced with the prospect of losing work-related benefits, and so he decided to sell his brainchild in 1989.

CONFLICT AND CONCERN

Word got out that S.O.S. was for sale, stoking discord among clubs in the association. Various entities showed much interest in taking over the S.O.S. Laughter, selecting the one with the most potential to succeed, chose the ACSC. This choice was unwelcome by some members, and considerable conflict ensued. A lack of cooperation and conflict also existed among the business interests in North Myrtle Beach.

In February 1989 the ACSC received an offer from Gene Laughter to purchase S.O.S. The board of advisers discussed the acquisition at the winter workshop in Mooresville, North Carolina, and without a dissenting vote approved the purchase.

On April 1, 1989, the ACSC took control of S.O.S., merging two organizations of immense importance to the future of the shagging world. The big fusion took place. Now the goal was to unify all and assure shaggers that the S.O.S. they loved so well would continue for many years.

A CATASTROPHE

During the Spring Safari the association held its first meetings of the S.O.S. with headquarters at Crazy Zack's, a disastrous decision. Only Zack's—and no other club—required the S.O.S. card. In some places card-burning parties took place accompanied by a festive atmosphere. The Spanish Galleon, which had been serving as the host club for Starbuck's Shagtime, seemed a logical choice for a headquarters. It wasn't. In its first start from the gate, the association lost thousands of dollars. Shaggers again found themselves disenfranchised by the British Invasion.

The problem came down to money, as it so often does. The Galleon had a large door of rock fans, especially on Friday and Saturday nights. At 10 o'clock the Galleon killed the beach music. Dressed to the nines, young rockers packed the place by the hundreds.

Shaggers liked to party late, and having nowhere to dance from 10:00 P.M. on didn't sit well with them. They were all dressed up with nowhere to go. For the Galleon, it was a business decision: go with the crowd that had been frequenting it.

Longtime treasurer Foster McKinney remembers the card fiasco:

> Sometime in May 1989, Larry Taylor, chairman of the S.O.S. board, asked me if I would be interested in serving as S.O.S. treasurer. He knew I was a certified public accountant. I was a mere novice at S.O.S. and told Larry I knew very little about it.
>
> "Don't worry, I'll show you the ropes," he said. I came on board, I believe, in June 1989. I was not there on board as an officer helping out at "Crazy Zack's" during our first S.O.S. the previous spring, but I was there

as a card-holding S.O.S. member. I could see people chewing on Dr. Phil Sawyer as I presented my S.O.S. card. He took the criticism graciously but held his ground. For a few years following that first Crazy Zack's debut, you'd been wise not to stand next to him because somebody would come up and chew on him about the crowds or anything else that gnawed at them. He made for a good sounding board.

The association set out to right the ship. The summer of 1989, unlike the utopian summers of legendary O.D. days, proved long and arduous. Sawyer and B. E. "Speedy" Lewis negotiated long and hard with club owners, who listened to the S.O.S. leadership because they believed their best interest lay with the association. Lewis, close to the club owners, opened a lot of doors when they most needed opening. To bring the Spanish Galleon into the S.O.S. family, the association agreed to compensate the club for any loss of income its exclusive beach music nights might cause. The S.O.S. board had agreed to treat all clubs equally, and the arrangement with the Spanish Galleon was extended to all clubs.

Harold Worley of the Spanish Galleon extended a warm welcome to S.O.S. cardholders in the September S.O.S. *Carefree Times*. He said that "he hoped to build a strong permanent relationship that can keep the shag in the O.D. area for many years to come."

Rock Carter, general manager of Little Duck's/Rock Option, also contributed a letter to the *Carefree Times*. It read, "At last! Coordination, cooperation, and peace at Ocean Drive. My hat's off to the Association of Carolina Shag Clubs for their success in saving a tradition none of us wanted to lose."

Harold Bessent wrote, "I have worked for the S.O.S. organization since day one. . . . The camaraderie that we have created during the past nine years has been due to membership and membership fees. . . . Since we now have the Spanish Galleon, Rock Option, Little Duck's Shag Club, and Fat Harold's at the Pad, I believe we will be better able to serve the S.O.S. membership." Bessent continued, thanking Phil Sawyer, B. E. "Speedy" Lewis, Butch Berry, and Bob Wood for their efforts to keep the S.O.S. together.

Allowing the Society of Stranders to dissolve wasn't an option as far as Sawyer and Wood were concerned. Indeed the conglomerate of Murl Augustine, Harold Bessent, Ken Hudspeth, Speedy Lewis, Joe Magee, Phil Sawyer, Larry Taylor, and Harold Worley had formed a crucial team that saved the S.O.S. Each man brought his skills to the enterprise.

Wood, a former president of ShagAtlanta and a 2003 Shagging Icon winner, had done much to promote the shag and to calm the troubled waters, as had allies Larry Taylor and Murl Augustine. Wood would do much to grow the association from 1990 to 1993. Augustine would go on to become a popular deejay known for "murling up" shaggers, and Taylor would serve as the first chairman of the S.O.S. board of directors.

These leaders and others returned solidarity to the S.O.S. One other vital result emerged from the Spring Safari disaster: membership cards were made more valuable. Cards now provided access to four clubs, food, easy mingling, crowd control, and peace and unity.

With agreements in place, the upcoming Fall Migration was a huge success, and the association boldly leaped into 1990. A multi-million-dollar success story took off.

Without the hard summer's work and agreements, S.O.S. would have gone bankrupt. Shaggers would have been relegated to reminiscing about the old days at O.D. and having no chance to live the dream again.

Of course problems persisted. Starbuck continued to be a thorn in the S.O.S.'s side. Even after the Association of Carolina Shag Clubs had purchased the S.O.S., the bad blood continued. In 1998 Starbuck agreed to cease holding his "Grand Party" events. He sent a five-page letter to S.O.S. officers complaining about the "suck-ass music" they encouraged and a litany of other petty issues, which he defended under a guise of keeping all things shag traditional. And then Starbuck's organization faded away.

Other distractions and challenges occurred. In the mid-1990s Mickey Reeves started an organization called Southern Shaggers Ltd., complete with a magazine, membership cards, and decals for car windows. The organization promoted its newsletter, a toll-free "1-800" service center, and a Web site. A good many shaggers joined S.O.S. and Southern Shaggers. Like T.A.P.S., Southern Shaggers had its last dance and faded away.

The ship, however, had been righted. Effective management, enlightened leadership, open administration of S.O.S. affairs, and a strong commitment from thousands of shaggers, Stranders, and beach music lovers ensured the continuance of S.O.S. Migrations, events people speak of today with holy overtones.

S.O.S. enjoyed unprecedented growth. Many features were added: trams, food, an expanded *Carefree Times,* line dance competition, the S.O.S. Beach Run, and Fun Monday. S.O.S. funds supported local club activities; the association took on a budget; and the Mid-Winter Beach Classic and charities began.

As with other vibrant organizations, challenges continued. In 2009 some shaggers expressed concern that some shag clubs were drifting from the shag, bringing other dances into the S.O.S. and other events held under the auspices of the ACSC and S.O.S. That didn't stop the media attention, though.

Atlantic Monthly, Smithsonian, and *Sandlapper* magazines covered shagging and the S.O.S. cultural phenomenon, as did South Carolina ETV. All this attention is about a dance and a fun-loving cult, the Society of Stranders. Nearly one hundred clubs, many in North and South Carolina, have ninety to seven hundred members each. Three annual events at O.D. (North Myrtle Beach) each draw more than fifteen thousand people.

The S.O.S. motto, "No Plans for Tomorrow," is simple, as all good mottoes are. That carefree spirit still flourishes, and the fun attracts other members to the society. They won't be lifeguards or hallowed beach bums, and they can't say they were at O.D. in the glory days, but they will do something important: they'll carry on the tradition of shagging to good music.

They'll pass on the lore and keep the memories of legendary O.D. alive. They'll dance, sip a while, party, make friends, and find lovers. After all, that is what started everything in the first place. Why should it be any different?

9

Love Letters in the Sand

*To be fond of dancing was a certain
step towards falling in love.*

Jane Austen,
Pride and Prejudice

Love blossomed to silken moves upon sandy floors as dancing and summer love fired up many a heart. Rhythmic movement and romance: that's the real love potion number 9.

The love came from the heart. Those ardent days at Ocean Drive were nothing like the hippies' stoned summer of love at Haight-Ashbury in 1967. With no war to protest and no agenda to pursue, shaggers were all about love and fun. The only drugs shaggers needed were cold beer and gushing hormones.

Shaggers didn't protest anything. They had no need for contraband, just good music. They demonstrated on sandy dance floors—showing how dance moves went, that is. For them it wasn't just one summer of love but many. If love didn't always work out, and sometimes it didn't, next summer might bring better luck. There'd be Carolina girls aplenty for all those Sixty Minute Men.

Hearts met shagging; hearts were broken shagging, and shaggers found love to be a wondrous, sometimes baffling alchemy. The aching, the beauty, the jubilation—they etched deep memories. For many shaggers, pining for a special summer of love became a cherished ritual. Longing, loving, and looking back . . .

"No matter where life took me, my mind lived back at Ocean Drive," said one woman who wishes to remain anonymous. Long a shagger, she had deeply loved the man she met on the dance floor one shimmering summer night. That was long ago. Though gone, he lives on in her memories. "I see him all the time, dancing," she said.

Yes, dear, and when the last dance ends, there's but one thing left to do. Have your ashes scattered at Ocean Drive.

OCEAN DRIVE had a name change, but the journey to love keeps ending in the same destination: that place by the sea. It's a happy journey, provided travelers pick their route carefully and fate smiles on them.

Life is but a sojourn, and alas, we are all sojourners. The journey takes us down familiar byways and roads to avoid, toll roads, you might say. For many there's a dead-end street to avoid at all costs, the Boulevard of Broken Dreams. It extracts a heavy price, and its travelers end up in a place named Heartache.

In 1942 Edward Hopper created one of American art's most recognizable paintings, *Nighthawks.* In the work a couple and a man sit at the bar of an all-night diner. The white-capped attendant is getting something from beneath the counter. What? We'll never know. The people have spent a long night out on the town. It's late. Very late. Something about that painting portrays loneliness, and if you've never seen it, you should.

"Unconsciously, probably, I was painting the loneliness of a large city," said Hopper. When you look at *Nighthawks,* you can't help but think of lonely people. The painting, if you look closely, portrays an all-night diner with no doors.

No way out. That's how many ill-starred women in their late forties and early fifties feel when they wake up one day adrift on the Boulevard of Broken Dreams. Their husbands have abandoned them in the prime of life, but not for another woman as the cliché goes. They died. Death might be the result of a heart attack, a stroke, or a car wreck; it depends on what fate had in mind. Life forced these women to begin anew, but alas, time is short.

"I never thought, at my age, that I'd be alone," one woman wrote. "I really didn't want to date again but I didn't want to be alone." Overnight life set her adrift on the boulevard, but she took a congenial exit to a place where happiness and acceptance dwell.

OVER FORTY AND SINGLE AGAIN

There's an acronym that goes with the shag culture; it's OFASA. Over forty and single again describes many people in the shag cult who find themselves single once again. The antidote to avoid being a nighthawk is companionship. OFASA is about satisfying the human craving for companionship. The shagging culture embraces people who've lost a long-term relationship, no matter the reason.

Shaggers' ages begin at about thirty-five and range into the seventies and eighties. The Spring and Fall Migrations include many people over forty and single again. This demographic group has different, more complex needs than the typical singles-bars clientele. Shag clubs, dances, and the annual Spring and Fall Migrations offer the OFASA a safe, acceptable way to enjoy life without the problems singles bars can bring.

Singles bars (the predictable "meat markets" to some) seldom lead to socializations that prove satisfactory to those over forty and single again. Regardless of their age or gender, people on their own again find the shag world a safe place to be single anew.

GREAT FUN AND GOOD MANNERS

Kay Hatcher has been single since 1993. She began shagging seriously in 1995 as she set out to make new friends and adjust to being single after twenty years of marriage and two children. Like other OFASA women, she liked what she saw in the shagging world.

"What I learned was that shaggers are a pretty tame group," said Kay. "They don't spill drinks all over the dance floor and leave broken glasses scattered around the bar. And I'm never worried about how many people might have a gun or a fight breaking out. At most shag bars, it would be hard to even know who the bouncer is, since, unlike some other types of bars, bouncers are not muscular tough guys walking around in black T-shirts that say 'bouncer' or 'security.'"

Nor has she seen a bouncer escort a shagger out the door. "Shag bars rarely need a bouncer, and that is what makes me very comfortable as a single female, as I often hop in my car and go alone," Kay said.

Another aspect of the shag world impressed Kay: shaggers dance with everyone. "Even the married couples like to dance with other people," she said. "Everyone knows a few different steps and has a little different style, so it's fun to dance the night away with lots of different partners. 'Would you like to dance?' is not a 'come on,' just an invitation to enjoy the dance we love so much. At most other types of bars, you would not dare ask another person's date or spouse to dance!"

GOT MY MOJO BACK

Pam Traugott has a story to tell. It's about her adjustments to being single after thirty-seven years of marriage. "It took a couple of years to begin to feel single again," she said. "I chose to dance and chose the shag as my dance. Now why I did this I am still not clear but it turned out to be a good choice. I started asking around and found a couple of single women who were willing to drive to various shag clubs. Thus began a journey toward friendship between us and learning the unspoken rules of the 'game.'"

The game has rules, which Traugott didn't know. "I felt like I had crawled out from under a rock. Ask a guy to dance? Are you kidding me? I had to learn how hard a guy has it and I had my share of refusals. I was a nervous wreck. I literally felt like I was walking around naked and nobody was looking at me. I now know I was just learning the ropes and I needed to relax. I had learned to shag in college but that was years ago and I didn't recognize any of the music that was now the Top 20. Where was 'My Girl?'"

Traugott said she had a lot to learn. She started taking shag lessons and going to dances. She was thankful when a guy would ask her to dance once or twice. She said, "While I might have thought I would find 'true love' on the dance floor, after four years of looking and dancing I realized that would be a rare happening. The dance itself has given me new friends, the confidence to ask anyone to dance. The shag community has helped me broaden my world."

Traugott doesn't hesitate to invite newly divorced ladies or widows to ride along with her and have some dance fun. "Like one of my girlfriends told me," she said, "'the dance has given you your mojo back.'"

A letter to *Carefree Times* expressed the gratitude of women who found themselves single again. "S.O.S. was my first social after my divorce and it coincided with my 40th birthday, so it had extra-special meaning to me and I know I speak for a good many others. To say again, as I am sure many before me have done, S.O.S. is magical! Twice a year we all head to our old playground, and for a few days, we are just Sylvia, Gene, Shirley, Sandra, Bob. Not someone's wife, mother, secretary. We are accepted just for our own face value and it's wonderful!"

THE SHAG DEVIL GOT ME

Carolyn Vaughan lost her husband, David, in September 2010. They had met at S.O.S. in 1989, fallen in love, and moved to Murrells Inlet. David was once a lifeguard at Ocean Drive. Today, she's ready to tell how at age fifty and single again, she's ready to tell how she found him:

> I was born in Greenville, South Carolina. When I was going into the tenth grade, Mama decided I should transfer out of my comfortable country school district into the elite side of town and go to Greenville High.
>
> There were some girls at church who went to Greenville High and I asked them a million questions that summer about the shag before tenth grade started. One Sunday, Evelyn Garlington showed me the basic shag step in the girls' bathroom and the obsession with dancing began. Some in my family would say the Shag Devil got me in the bathroom of the Bible Presbyterian Church.
>
> The dance floors were fertile for the shag in the mid-1950s. Beach bums, beach regulars, and beach workers came home after Labor Day and "lowered themselves" to teaching hometown girls to dance. My new crowd of friends at Greenville High included Rowena Melton who was the best friend forever to end all best friends forever—not only did she have her own car but she could watch a couple do a new step and count it out for the rest of us. Rowena made us into possible dance partners—a much-desired status at the teen canteen after football games.
>
> At some point, we attracted the attention of Beaver Greenway and David Smith, local boys, but summer beach bums with a soul infected with the Shag Devil. They seemed to think we had potential.
>
> David was born in Florence, an only child whose family ran a grocery store. A typical Southern boy, he grew up camping, hunting, and fishing. It seems that girls discovered him and he discovered girls and this new activity curtailed his outdoor activities. He was drop-dead gorgeous and had a muscled body that did not come from lifting weights. He also had that most admired attribute in this era—he was just "cool."

David told me that some girl in Florence taught him to dance and that made him into the perfect package. The summer of 1956 he went to the beach to work for the summer. He got a job as a "monkey," a gofer for the lifeguards.

In 1958 he was a guard, living in the lifeguard's house, a half-block behind the Pad with meals cooked for him and extras provided by the girls who were down on house parties. He stayed on the beach all day, getting brown and meeting girls. Then, he walked to the guardhouse, ate a home-cooked meal, showered, and changed into a crisply ironed shirt and shorts (by some lucky girl with an iron) and made his entrance at the Pad. Brown, even between his toes, coiffed, broad shoulders, small hips, blond crew cut, starched button down, bad to the bone, naturally cool David Vaughan walked into his world.

Vaughan said she witnessed that entrance the first week in June 1958 while at a house party following graduation from Greenville High.

More than thirty years later, their worlds merged at S.O.S. in 1989. Both realized it was a magical meeting. David had never been to S.O.S., in part out of contempt for those who were trying to recapture what was there at an earlier time. Carolyn Vaughan had been to almost every one, chasing the Shag Devil. This meeting of a "wannabe shagger," as she described herself, and a real beach lifeguard lasted twenty years until he, body worn by partying, just couldn't go on. Vaughan is thankful for the time they had.

STEPS TOWARD LOVE

Among the special memories are those of the bold. In a reversal of shag fortunes, girls sometimes taught the boys steps, and the steps sometimes led to the altar . . . well not an altar per se, as Joan Bassett's memory reveals, but the result was the same. Bassett said, "Sid Fritts from Lexington, North Carolina, was my first husband whom I met in the Pad, which was the smallest, darkest, dance place on the beach. It was truly the beginning juke joint at North Myrtle Beach. My sister, Kay Cameron, who was 10 years older, hung out there in 1955. I was in there one night when Sid asked me to dance. I was 19 and so was he."

"Sid was a lifeguard, 6 feet 4 inches, 210 pounds, blond, tanned, and gorgeous," said Joan. "Up to this point in my life I only dated the small ugly boys who could dance. So I guess at 19 my hormones were kicking in and I decided to try something new: kissing instead of dancing."

Joan taught Sid a lot of her steps, and he became a pretty good dancer "for his height." He attended Wingate College, and she was going to the University of North Carolina in the fall.

"I hung out at his lifeguard stand and we dated every night that summer," said Joan. "When I started at the University of North Carolina I was in Chapel Hill and Sid was near Charlotte but we took turns going to see each other. We went to spend the weekend with his parents at the end of September and decided to run away and get married in York, South Carolina."

Joan and Sid got married and went to a shag club in Charlotte before going back to his parents' house. "His mom found out we had gotten married in York and insisted we get married in the church," said Joan. "I said my dad would never agree to spend all that money with me married already."

Sid got her a ring and gave it to her at the beach in a romantic live oak grove in O.D. That grove is now full of condos.

"We got married at the Baptist church in Chapel Hill and had the reception at the Carolina Inn with 300 people and a champagne fountain. The other two couples who were in our wedding got married too and they are still together."

In an interview with Johanna D. Wilson, a writer with *TheSunNews.com,* both Ron Whisenant and Tom Barrineau, S.O.S. officers, alluded to the shag's romantic potential:

> Any man who shags, they both said, knows he's a man who has the ability to pick up good-looking, good-dancing women.
>
> "Girls," Whisenant said. "That's why I started shagging, to meet girls. If any other shaggers tell you different, they are lying because their wives are right beside them." Back in 1962 in Charlotte, Whisenant met his wife, Peggy, at a shag event.

That was almost fifty years ago.

Love blossomed and lasted for many, but for some the sweetest, most tender, most beautiful flowers died too quickly, as one anonymous shagger's memoir sadly chronicles.

"SHE WAS MY QUEEN"

The anonymous shagger's memoir reads as follows:

> This particular night was like no other; I walked into the club and made my way through the packed club to the back deck. I stood at the top of the

crowded stairway looking down at the jam-packed dance floor. I looked to my right then to my left and there she was.

She stood out in the crowd of hundreds. She was like a bright light shinning in the darkness. Her blonde hair glowed. She was in an all-black pants outfit. Her smile was the most beautiful smile I had ever seen.

A song began to play. The name of the song was "8-3-1": Eight letters, three words, one meaning, "I Love You."

As soon as the song began to play, I heard her soft tender voice say, "I love that song. I wish someone would ask me to dance." As she spoke those words, she turned her head to the right. Our eyes met. Without saying a word I pointed to her with my right index finger, then I pointed to me, and then to the dance floor.

She began to move toward me and me toward her. It was like we were in slow motion. Our hands reached out for each other. I escorted her to the dance floor. I held her for a few seconds before I started to dance. She melted in my arms. I had butterflies in my stomach. Who was this woman who made me feel as though I was young again?

We danced the rest of the night. I didn't want to let her go. When the clock struck 2 A.M. it was time to leave.

The next night she was there waiting for me. We danced the whole night. She looked into my eyes as no other woman has. Our hearts connected. We danced as though we were one. Even though it was so crowded, we danced like there was no one else on the floor.

She was my dance partner on the floor and in my heart. I was her knight in shining armor. She was my queen.

We sat on the bench on 2nd Ave until the early morning just talking. I fell in love with her the moment I saw her.

We dated for two years and got married. The theme song at our wedding was "8-3-1." We danced and danced. I was the happiest I have ever been in my life.

We were married for three years. The irony of this story is that the old clubs they are gone and so is she, but the memories remain dear to my heart.

POLISHING THE APPLE

The annals of love are filled with men and women who stretch the truth now and then. As they say, all's fair in love and war. Charlotte Moore of Lexington, Virginia, learned that when it comes to boys impressing girls, little white lies were to be expected. "When I first began going to S.O.S. I was advised to not believe everything a guy tells you," said Charlotte.

She knew a person could meet his or her true love, leading to something substantial and permanent, but she knew too that didn't often happen. "The time was for fun and fantasy and especially to dance," she said, "fantasy" being a key word.

"Guys seem to embellish a little on their professional life. I was chatting with a couple of guys between dances one night when one told me he was an assistant coach for a well-known NFL football team." Charlotte's reply was, "Let's see now, you say you are a pro-team coach, so I would guess you are coaching for a local high school team." Annoyed, he turned to his buddy and said, "You told her!" They all had a good laugh.

Charlotte knows all too well that guys aren't the only ones who polish their own apple when it comes to making an impression. She said:

> I was chatting with this guy. In fact, we were getting rather chummy, when he asked me how old I was. Now, I take pride that I can pass for being 10 years younger than I am, so I told him I was 52. Later, we were discussing how much fun retiring would be. I slipped and said something about receiving Social Security.
>
> He looked blank and said, "If you are 52 how are you receiving Social Security?"

That was a big "oops" moment for Charlotte, who confessed, "We gals can embellish too, and usually it is about our age." She paused and added, "which guys should not be asking about anyway."

AGE IS JUST A NUMBER

The truth is, age matters little among shaggers. Joan Kimbro, president of the Burlington Shag Club, addressed the issue of age and more. Her hope is that once people have tended to their families, careers, and other life demands, they can get back out and enjoy life.

Kimbro said, "As kids ourselves, we, too, had lots of friends and enjoyed lots of parties, but after we grew up so to speak, we found new obligations. Years would pass and before we knew it we had stopped being that kid."

People change, people grow, and sometimes the growth and changes fracture relationships. "Often couples would grow apart because life took them in different directions," said Kimbro. "They shared the same home but one day realized they were not on the same page. That is where a group of our friends were 25 years ago. Thank goodness one lady decided to start a shag club that allowed both partners to do something they had once enjoyed together."

Kimbro said that the word spread and women, especially, encouraged their husbands to check out the club. An amazing thing happened.

"People remembered the steps and that music and found instant youth again. Friends found friends again, made new friends, and realized that kid was still inside dying to get out. It didn't matter if you had gained weight or lost some hair," Kimbro explained.

More people came, and each week people gathered and became close friends again. That old safe harbor OFASA again worked its magic.

"Women or men who no longer had a partner came also," said Kimbro. "They had had problems starting over, but in this world, or as we say, the shag lifestyle, all are welcome. Clubs were forming all around us and soon these groups started visiting each other, thus there was [*sic*] more ways to meet new people. Age is not an issue," she said, alluding to kids and shaggers in their nineties. "On the dance floor we are all equal."

What matters is reconnecting and having fun.

THOSE WERE THE DAYS

A 1988 edition of *Carefree Times* carried a feature, "Back to the Beach," a reprint from the April 16, 1988, *Greensboro News and Record*. That feature carried a subhead, "Looking for Love." Beneath that subhead, Janie Bolin looked back on the summers of 1957 through 1960 at Ocean Drive. In an offhand way she referred to something back then that remains true today: "Marry in haste; repent at leisure."

"I don't want to go back to those times," wrote Bolin, "but it's fun to be with so many people your own age. A lot of these people got married right out of high school. Now they're divorced and going back to the old places, the same ones where they met their first mates. It's like you're already friends with everybody. That makes it so easy." Easy indeed to meet people with whom you share a lot in common.

Bert and Brenda Sanford wrote a short but sweet letter to *Carefree Times* in 1986. It read: "Here's our S.O.S. application. The last names are now the same. We met last March at S.O.S. and have been inseparable ever since. We were married February 7, 1986. Thanks for S.O.S. It has made a wonderful difference in our lives."

Many shaggers met, fell in love, and married. Wayne Bennett's wife, Judy, was a regular to S.O.S. starting in 1990. A charter member of the Golden Isles Shag Club in Brunswick, Georgia, today she's a Shagging Icon.

"We met at Mid-Winter in 2003 on the floor at Ducks," said Wayne, "and married a little over a year later." It could easily not have happened. Judy had told her friends she wasn't going to Mid-Winter that year but did after her two best friends prodded her to go. It was there that a mutual friend introduced them. "She met me and the rest is history," said Wayne. Today, Wayne and Judy teach shag in Brunswick, Georgia, and Wayne deejays for the club. And they continue to do what brought them together: dance twice a week.

Foster McKinney met his wife, Teri, in Columbia at Butch's Beach Club, owned and operated by renowned beach and shag deejay Butch Davidson. Foster had been shagging for a little over a year after taking lessons from Hall of Famers Norman and Wanda Holliday.

Foster said, "I'd occasionally drop in on Norman and Wanda's shag lessons to lend a willing and able pair of male feet to accompany soloing female students. And then in the winter of 1988, there she stood." "She" was Teri, a woman taking lessons with a longtime friend who had recently lost her daughter in a tragic accident. Teri felt she needed to get her friend's mind occupied with a hobby that would put her in the company of others.

"I was fortunate enough to pair up with Teri in helping with her basic step," said Foster. "When I first touched her hand, sparks flew. It was an unmistakable, true feeling that said 'this feels right.'"

Teri and Foster dated for a little over two years, and then at the 1990 S.O.S. Spring Safari, Foster proposed to Teri. "We were at Fat Harold's Beach Club, at the Pad. Our good friend, Bill Kelly, later the S.O.S. photographer, leaned in right beside me and waited for a response. After what felt like an eternity, she said 'yes.'"

Bill rushed straight for the deejay booth and had the house deejay, Gary Bass, announce it over the loud speakers. Foster and Teri were married that year on September 22, 1990.

"Experts had told Teri she was unlikely to ever bear children," said Foster, "but shortly after we were married we had two boys. We have been happy together ever since I touched her hand at Butch's Beach Club. I vividly remember my very first shag lesson when Norman Holliday told us the 'shag will change your life.' It definitely changed mine, much for the better."

The shag changed Helen and Rodney Still's life for the better too. "I remember when I was growing up doing all the fad dances," said Helen, "but

I loved to do the old beach shag. The beach shag was what I knew for many years. When Rodney and I met he was not a dancer, except slow dancing. I felt like we were in an old folks home, because I wanted to shag. I would have to meet my girlfriends at the beach and go out to see if we could find someone to dance with."

Helen kept begging Rodney to let her show him the steps. Finally, after twelve years of marriage, they were down at the beach, and he let her show him the steps.

"All I had with me was my walkman, so I turned it wide open so he could hear the music," said Helen. They went dancing that night. "The next year we were introduced to the Carolina shag and converted to the more structured style of dancing. Rodney is now a DJ—what a difference the music and the shag have made in our lives."

WERE IT NOT FOR THE SHAG

The shag connected people inland, far from the beach, and in one case it connected a couple in more ways than romantic ones. That was the case with Anne and Allen Henry. Anne's story, like those of other shaggers, tells of a chance meeting inland at one of the S.O.S. workshops.

"Back in the early 1990s, I was living in Jacksonville, Florida, where we were just beginning to have organized shag lessons," said Anne. "Being the 'worker bee' I am, I jumped in to help Kelly Cordell form the First Coast Shag Club, prepare bylaws, and apply to the Association of Carolina Shag Clubs. On the second weekend in 1992—July 10, to be exact—a good friend of mine, Becky, called to tell me she had heard about a workshop being held in Charlotte, and that we should go."

Anne, being a bit shy, served up a list of excuses. When she ran out of excuses, she agreed to go, and off they went. "I was pretty much of a wallflower at that point in time but Becky would pick out dancers she wanted to dance with and off she would go," said Anne. "On Saturday night, July 11, she picked out one Allen Henry who was at the workshop with a group representing ShagAtlanta."

Becky brought Allen over to Anne, and the rest is history. "We dated long distance for a while and married in February 1994."

Anne moved from Jacksonville to Atlanta, where Allen lived, and they began a new lifestyle at fifty-something. Having overcome her shyness, she became ShagAtlanta's president, while Allen served as treasurer. Allen would become treasurer of the ACSC in 1997, a position he holds to this day.

"In 1999, I was approached about being appointed as executive secretary of the Society of Stranders," said Anne. She held that position until 2004. "We not only gained new (non-paying) jobs but a family whom we love dearly," Anne continued. "We both retired during this time and I was missing my friends and family in Jacksonville. Allen agreed to relocate to Florida. We returned to First Coast Shag Club, where, after several years as treasurer, I now serve as president and Allen as membership chair."

Anne and Allen hold the distinct honor of being Shagging Icons. However, were it not for the shag, neither their romance nor their illustrious shag history might have come to pass.

A DANCE WITH SPILLANE AND MORE

Peggy Ann Wrenn has lived in North Myrtle Beach since April 1990. Her parents had lived there since 1978. To say she was exposed to the shag is an understatement. She always wanted to shag, but her husband at the time didn't want any part of it.

"Mom used to bring us down to the Pad and Fat Harold's on the Ocean and watch people dance," said Peggy Ann. "When I turned 40, life with my husband changed, and we ended our marriage. So I went to Duck's with my neighbor, Denise Puckett, and we took shag lessons. I enjoyed my new life, new friends, and dancing."

She decided to go to S.O.S., which brought a lot of joy into her life. It brought a great surprise as well. A silver-haired man dressed in black, a former lifeguard from Breezy Point, Queens, New York, approached her. "My first dance was with Mickey Spillane. I had no clue who I was dancing with, I was just thrilled someone asked me to dance!"

That was in the 1980s. Years later, in 2003, Peggy Ann met a wonderful man during S.O.S. at H's, a short-lived club where Crazy Zack's was, and two years later, on June 25, 2005, she married again. "If I hadn't got out and danced, I would have never met my wonderful husband," Peggy Ann said.

Some couples have not only met as shaggers but also married as shaggers. As an S.O.S. officer and president emeritus, Phil Sawyer has married close to a dozen shag couples. Harold Bessent has married shag couples, as has retired judge John Breland, who shags.

Several weddings have taken place during S.O.S., but the Morgans' was the first marriage scheduled as an S.O.S. event. Sawyer gave the bride away at the OD Arcade.

"Camille and I had a traditional wedding in 1992 complete with shag bridesmaids, groomsman, shag minister and DJ," said Bruce Morgan. "A large crowd of the S.O.S. family attended as part of S.O.S. events. Governor Campbell even issued a proclamation for 'September 19th—Bruce and Camille Morgan Day.'"

ROMANCE

People love heartwarming stories about how couples met. And the couples themselves long look back on how they met. The craving to recapture youth and love? It's human to long for the past, and shaggers have quite a past. With a bit of money in their pockets and no more war to endure, young people succumbed to beach fever. As the years flew by, couples kept meeting, and the memories accumulated.

Unhurried days on the beach and nights of romance stamped indelible memories into the minds of many. They'd never forget walking hand in hand along the surf, the old pavilions, and dance halls. Nor would they fail to recall nights of cold beer, neon Wurlitzers, Rock-Olas, Seeburgs, great music, and love. These made for sentimental memories.

"SENTIMENTAL JOURNEY"

In 1944, just about the time the shag was set to launch, Doris Day recorded "Sentimental Journey." Members of a cult would make their own sentimental journey someday. Swink Laughter did.

Some three decades after the 1950 glory days, Laughter, in a column in the *Carefree Times*, sounded lovesick for the old days when couples strolled by the sea:

What happened to those brisk cool night breezes from the sea?

Maybe the high-rise condos and plastic, chrome and glitter have screened them off?

Oh, we had a few hot, still nights when we had to go out on the beach and sleep on a float, but normally we were very comfortable clad in our summer woolens. . . .

Yeah, those were the days.

It's really hard to fathom just how little we had. Yet we had so much— so much love and so much fun!

All that fun and love left their mark on people and on literature. In *Beach Music,* Pat Conroy's main character, Jack McCall, wants his daughter, Leah, to better appreciate her southern heritage. His solution is southern: he introduces her to the shag and classic beach music. He brings up the Drifters' immortal song "Save the Last Dance for Me," telling her, "This is your Mama's and my favorite song. We fell in love dancing to it."

They weren't the only ones. For many a man and woman, the shag was a signpost to a beautiful boulevard, a lovers' lane where dreams came true.

10

The Music

*To stop the flow of music would be like the stopping
of time itself, incredible and inconceivable.*

Aaron Copland,
The Pleasures of Music

Like the dancers who love it, beach music today is organized and formally promoted, a far cry from Ocean Drive's days when kids sneaked off to hear race music.

Kids used to steal over to Whispering Pines to hear the music at Charlie's Place. Now the music, its makers, and dancers have traveled the long road to mainstream acceptance. The race line was crossed long ago. Music built a bridge between the races, and Charlie's Place has long been rendered obsolete. B. B. King might as well sing "The thrill is gone," for the danger faded as race relations improved and fights with soldiers withered, then died.

But controversy lives on. Like so many aspects of the shag's history, the music serves up an area where people differ. Some are adamant as to what beach music is; others are more flexible. The debate today is, "what is beach music?"

In the early days no one ever heard the term "beach music." They heard terms such as "race music," R&B, and "Chitlin Circuit" music. Gene Laughter described it as "down-home, funky, sweaty, loud, shouting, cooking, rocking, chicken-shack, gospel-inspired Negro boogie, and blues." He wasn't referring, he said, to the "pretty, lily-white, blue-eyed, Anglo-Saxon Embers and Catalina variety of 'Beach Music' with cute lyrics about the sea, sun, and suds."

Along the beaches, wrote Laughter, "this suggestive negro music could be heard at the many white teenage dance pavilions that dotted the coast. Slowly a following of white fans developed that eventually grew into a cult, of sorts—a lifestyle!"

He also wrote about how the phrase "rock and roll" kept popping up in the lyrics of R&B tunes. This expression, he wrote, was "black jive talk for 'making love.' It got right down to the nitty gritty!"

Then things changed. The British Invasion brought a new kind of "rock and roll" to America. "A new generation went crazy over rock and roll," wrote Laughter, "without ever knowing what the expression really meant. Black R&B recording artists must have split their sides in laughter when white DJs started screaming the Negro slang expression for fornicating, 'Rock and Roll,' over the very same air waves that had earlier banned their music because of its suggestive lyrics."

The love for the old music goes a ways back, and there's dispute as to *where* the music took hold. Johnie Davis and his fellow Cape Fear Shag Club members take a strict traditionalist approach to the shag and its old music. "In the late 1950s, when Cherry Grove and Ocean Drive had places like the Pad and Sonny's Pavilion, the highway system from the inland cities made travel to O.D. easier than to Carolina Beach. It got real popular down there, but the music started here (Carolina Beach). It was old blues music," said Davis, "whose club dances to the old blues tunes, not the newer beach tunes. We danced to 'These Blues is Killing Me' by the Ravens. 'Juke Box' by Gene Pitney. 'Shut Yo Mouth' by B. B. King. Our philosophy is the DJs don't play anything made after 1955" (from *Livin' Out Loud* magazine, June 2010, with permission from Nancy Hall Publications).

In one of the 80.8 million Google results for the term "beach music," Wikipedia describes beach music, or Carolina beach music, as a regional genre that developed from the "raucous sounds of blues/jump blues, reggae, rockabilly and old-time rock and roll" and is "closely associated with the style of swing dance known as the shag, or the Carolina shag" (from *Livin' Out Loud* magazine, June 2010, with permission from Nancy Hall Publications).

As the end of the 1980s approached, deejays drifted away from the beach music standards of the 1950s and 1960s. They pushed new blues tunes, and that irked old-line shaggers who preferred the hits of the Tams, the Drifters, the Platters, the Ravens, the Clovers, Earl Bostic, Ruth Brown, Wynonie Harris, and others. Some shaggers felt that the deejays were showing off their musical knowledge. A lot of folks complained about the new music.

In January 1987 a Raleigh deejay wrote a letter to *Carefree Times* bemoaning the direction the music was taking:

> Really enjoy the S.O.S. weekends and I share your concern for the direction that "Beach" music is taking. Blues is OK for a diversion. . . . Country I can tolerate . . . but "Beach" they ain't. As a DJ who plays a great deal of Beach on the air and at private parties, and before that in clubs, I believe that some of the DJs are simply following the lead of a few, i.e. S.P.A. dancers, that can only hear with their feet! They have created a whole new genre of music . . . "Shag" music which is OK to play at contests . . . but at gatherings like S.O.S., you have a great many people that only come to the beach for the gathering each year. They don't know or care what the hottest record on the circuit is—they want to hear what they remember from their youth, their carefree times.

That letter wasn't unique. Other shaggers wrote in requesting to hear the music of their youth. Shaggers didn't like the dance contests and songs that "were never popular and never will be." They thirsted for the songs they associated with O.D. of the 1950s and 1960s: Earl Bostic, Wynonie Harris, Ruth Brown, the Clovers, Roy Brown, Joe Turner, Tiny Bradshaw, the Drifters, and others. "Save the weird blues stuff for contests and tourists," wrote one dissenter.

In the next issue of *Carefree Times,* a deejay from Columbia responded to those complaining about the songs his colleagues were playing: "As for 'Shag Music' this runs the gauntlet from early R&B to 60's and 70's soul music . . . to disco shag . . . to country shag . . . to top 40's stuff. If it has the right beat, why not? Does the shag music have to be from a certain era? Does it also have to be 'Beach Music'? One letter mentioned, 'It's not beach music and never will be.' That's why I prefer to call it 'Shag Music.' It's all good music and, if it's danceable, go to it! Maybe I've shed some light on why more of the 'standards' are not heard [at] S.O.S. functions. I personally would like to hear more of them and I'm not afraid to play them as long as there is dance response. Maybe it's time for the pendulum to swing back the other way. Let's hope so."

Around 1986 Swink Laughter had written in *Carefree Times* that beach music was peaking out. He wrote, "The newness of rebirth is gone. Shag contests are passé." He told one reader who had written him, "The movement has been over-hyped. Ask some of the beach club owners about their bottom lines for this year. I'm afraid some clubs may change their musical formats over the coming year or two . . . I feel that we have already seen the crest of the beach music wave. Time will tell."

Was Laughter right? Did the music lose its way? Or are we just forgetful?

TIME OBSCURES THINGS. Dust rains down on our memories, and the origins of the music grow dimmer year by year. The people who helped create it are dying, and their descendants forget or fail to learn where the music came from. But that doesn't stop the music. The music lives on albeit in a more structured way.

Today the deejays are organized, the bands have Web sites, the music has Web sites, and there's a Beach Music Association International whose mission is to broaden beach music's appeal. There's even an organization that gives annual beach music awards akin to the Grammys.

From the Atlantic Seaboard to *Billboard,* people define shag music, that old race music, that old whatever it was, in different ways. Which B to B or not to B, that is the question when defining shag music. This music fits into categories all starting with the letter "B."

It sprang from the blues, and then some referred to it as "boogie" music. Some blacks referred to it as "blue" music. Then the "beach" tag stuck, but now if you ask shaggers what true beach music is *not,* you'll hear yet another term that sounds a bit disdainful: bubblegum music.

David Sessoms wrote an insightful feature when he was secretary of the Association of Beach and Shag Club DeeJays. In "Just What Is Shag Music?" Sessoms tackled the terms used to describe the music. He wrote, "There are a lot of terms that are used loosely out there to describe the music (or subsets of it) that we (shaggers) dance to and occasionally sip a few beers to. These include 'Shag Music,' 'Beach Music,' 'Smoothies,' 'Boogie Woogie,' 'Bubblegum,' and even 'Tourist Beach Music,' which, of course, all true shaggers loathe!" Sessoms went on to say that none of these terms mean the same thing to any two shaggers.

He addressed the bewildering points of view as to what constitutes true shag music: "In fact, there is such a variety of types of music out there that is enjoyed by different people or regions, although they are all legitimate shaggers, that I am firmly convinced that if a DJ were to compile a list of 100 proven and well-known shag songs, and then ask 10 well-versed shaggers to select their 10 favorite songs, that they would generally be in agreement on about

20 percent of their selections. And there is nothing wrong with that! That is one of the great things about shag music, there is something out there for everybody."

The debate rages. Ask most anyone what beach music is, and chances are you'll get a different response. Some will say it is band music from groups such as the Tams.

Age plays a factor in the debate. Some shaggers take a hard line, insisting that only hardcore R&B is true shag music. A shagger with memories of the early 1950s music might tell you that today's bands play bubblegum beach. To a lot of veteran shaggers, the old R&B that black artists created is true shag music.

The beat reigns all-important. If a song comes in around 120 beats a minute, you can shag to it. In "The Infinite Shag," the *Independent Weekly*'s July 26, 2006, cover story, Chris Toenes wrote, "In fact, it can be argued that there are no 'beach music bands' because most party bands don't exclusively play beach music. If shag can be said to have a defining characteristic, it's a rhythmic range just above and below 120 beats per minute. The drummer must drop into that rhythmic pocket and stay there for the maximum 'shagability,' a common element of groups playing this music."

Delbert McClinton's "Mess o' Blues" proved that people could shag to music that defied a purist "beach music" definition, and all that did was muddy the picture. How best to define "pure" beach music? What if you graphically portray the evolution of the music? What if you pinned up every song ever shagged to by its copyright date across a huge wall? Could you unravel the time line and clearly pinpoint shag music's evolution with certainty?

The next time you go to Home Depot or Lowe's, go over to the interior paint section swatches and pretend that every hue, every tint you see is a shag song placed by copyright. The musical cousins line up neat and pretty. Notice how the colors ever so gradually change, but change they do. By the time you work your way to the rack's far side, you're nowhere near where you started. Perhaps that is the best way to visualize what happened to beach music.

Don't feel alone if you can't classify beach music songs with confidence. So much change has transpired that beach music's roots in rhythm and blues are lost even on the very race that created it. Frank Beacham in "Charlie's Place" quoted Maurice Williams of Maurice Williams and the Zodiacs on this fact. "The beginning of beach music was predominantly rhythm and blues," said Williams, "but today if you say to a young black man, 'come on, let's go and listen to a beach music show,' he'll say 'I ain't going to that white music.' The average black kid in his twenties or thirties doesn't know what this is all about. They see a beach music festival and think it's all white music. It's strange. They haven't studied the history of their music and the guys who recorded it enough to know what beach music is all about. They just don't know any better."

Beacham also wrote about the music's "beach music" label, quoting the late General Johnson in *Frank Beacham's Journal: Musings on Music, Culture, Technology, and History* (www.frankbeacham.com):

> General Johnson knew his history and understood the resistance to black music from the Ku Klux Klan and Southern leaders following World War II. But he also understood the unspoken attraction of Southern white kids to black music.
>
> "The average person of the Caucasian race could not listen to that music because it was blue music . . . if you listened to blue music you were scorned," Johnson told me. "But that same music was on the jukeboxes down in Myrtle Beach. And . . . if you listened to John R (on WLAC in Nashville) you could go down to Myrtle Beach and nobody looked down on you. That's basically why it's called beach music—though it was actually rhythm and blues."

The raw attraction of white kids to black performers, Johnson said, could be summed up in one word: feeling. "Black artists were able to communicate the feeling of the song they were singing both lyrically and musically. You can call it soul or whatever, but basically it is feeling," he said.

CALL IT WHAT YOU WILL

You can call it what you want, all right. To be sure, the music changed and the means by which to play it changed. From the old 45- and 78-rpms it evolved into eight-tracks, cassettes, CDs, and now iPods and downloadable files from the Internet. Black bands and black performers gave way to deejays and beach music bands, many of which are white.

People will always differ on how they define beach music, and that often depends on *when* they were exposed to the music. In "Shuffling on Main Street, S.O.S. Fall Migration 2000," Tim Bullard wrote that Ron Whisenant had a controversial opinion regarding the debate on beach music, which has at least two dominant camps. Whisenant said, "I have some mixed emotions about some of the music we play. I came along with some of the stuff they call 'Bubble Gum Music.'"

Harry Turner, president of the Beach Music Association International, described beach music as "a combination of rhythm and blues, the blues, the Motown sound, good-time rock 'n' roll and doo-wop."

Regardless of how some define it, the music has escaped those days when to listen to it was to court disaster. It's celebrated today and has its own awards.

The Carolina Beach Music Awards (CBMA Awards, first called the Cammys for "Carolina's Magic Music Years") began in 1995 in Salisbury, North Carolina. Charlotte, a shag hotbed, provided the CBMA a home for the next two years. In 1998 the CBMAs moved to North Myrtle Beach.

The Carolina Beach Music Academy arose from suggestions from industry professionals and beach music fans. According to the CBMA Web site, "The CBMA Awards promote Carolina Beach Music, its influences and offshoots and the unique Carolina lifestyle through the presentation of an awards show each November in North Myrtle Beach."

The show honors winners in various categories and, just as important, remembers the music's pioneers. Awards honor performers, songwriters, radio personalities, mobile DJs, dancers, producers, engineers, promoters, and others involved with the music's success. An overriding goal is to keep beach music alive.

Another organization promotes the music: folks who spin the records. The Association of Beach and Shag Club DeeJays preserves and promotes beach and shag music and their associated lifestyles. Their worldview encompasses the "beach and shag" lifestyle and includes the shag dance, beach and shag gatherings, shag dance contests, junior shagger events, and more. These deejays man the frontline where shaggers request songs. They're the ones who "watch the floor" at parties, S.O.S. dances, and other events. Their 2010 "Top 50 Shag Songs" list reveals just how much more open "beach music" is today; contemporary artists sit side by side with perennial favorites.

THE BEACH MUSIC HALL OF FAME

In September 2009 Coastal Carolina University announced that it would house the International Beach Music Hall of Fame to recognize the importance of "beach music," the genre of rhythm and blues music associated with the Grand Strand's culture and lifestyle. Plans came together in May 2009 when the South Carolina General Assembly passed a resolution designating Coastal Carolina University as "the home of the Beach Music Hall of Fame."

Harry Turner, president of the Beach Music Association International, spearheaded the university's affiliation with beach music. The Carolina Beach

Music Association also supports the Hall of Fame project at Coastal Carolina University.

The music gets its share of support, and regardless of what people prefer or define as beach music, in the Southeast the old music still runs strong. Songs on a list of beach-music favorites can be more than forty years old, and yet new songs continue to come. Shagger and dance instructor Ellen Taylor commented on the music, noting that whatever it is, it isn't static: "The music is constantly changing. Not only are the shaggers dancing to rhythm and blues, they are dancing to country, Latin, hip-hop, disco, contemporary, classic, all genres of music." As Sessoms said, "One of the great things about shag music is there's something out there for everybody."

In Appendix B you'll find several lists of favored shag songs. The lists reflect varied tastes, opinions, and frequency of requests. It doesn't matter if you agree with the rankings or the inclusions, what matters are the memories these songs resurrect. See if you can go through the list without singing along and conjuring up "a mess o' great memories."

Let the great music debate rage on. Long may the great river that is the shag flow . . .

11

Into the Future

May the dreams of your past be the reality of your future.

Anonymous

The dream that propelled young people to dance on the heels of World War II flourished, and then it began to die, or so it seemed. It's hard to keep a good dance down. The dance that brought the races together in music, the dance that Elvis and the British Invasion and disco tried to kill, lives on, and today it is spreading out from its southern roots.

Varying influences have helped the shag expand. Several, in particular, have introduced the dance to new geography and new generations: the spread of shag clubs; the organizing of young shaggers; the advent of shag instructors; and dance competition.

JUNIORS DANCE INTO THE FUTURE

"Give us your bald, your gray, your masses of former beach bums yearning to be free." This pronouncement ran in the S.O.S Spring Safari 1986 program. Today that decree merits an addendum: "Give us your locks, curls, manes, and tresses, your young and limber, your masses of future dancers." While some young people view the shag as a dance long out of vogue, it does appeal to other young people.

Joan Kimbro, president of the Burlington Shag Club, finds that some of today's younger set dance to something she doesn't recognize. She said, "I went to a wedding and watched the young kids dance—I guess that's what they were doing, there was music being played at any rate. I thought, now this dance will not last very long."

Kimbro knows of what she speaks. "From the time I was 13 and now 63, I am still doing the same dance I learned at Lloyds Swimming Pool at the dance hall. I still listen to the same songs I sang when I was 13. Most important, those songs had actual words and real heartfelt meanings."

Kimbro attended an S.O.S. Mid-Winter Break and watched the juniors dance. "I was brought to tears," she said. "The shag is not just a dance; it is a lifestyle. It has meaning and purpose and, as I witnessed at Mid-Winter, it brings all ages to the same table."

At Mid-Winter she watched as a thirteen-year-old boy danced with a lady close to her age. "It was pure beauty as each age was bringing the same dance steps alive," she remarked:

> There was no generation gap visible, just pure pleasure at being able to dance with a partner who shared the love for the music.
>
> I hope to be dancing till my time comes to leave this world. I love the dance and am so thankful for the young juniors who are keeping this alive for us.

Kimbro takes solace in what the S.O.S. is doing. More than a quarter-century later, the S.O.S. shares its love for the shag and heartfelt songs with young people.

These young dancers are referred to as "junior" shaggers, shaggers under twenty-one years of age. Junior shaggers have their own organization, the Junior Shag Association. Its goal is simple: to promote and perpetuate beach and shag dance music and shagging. True to the shag's origins, the association participates in fun events that allow members the opportunity to showcase their mastery of the shag's intricacies.

The Junior Shag Association, for instance, holds fun contests during Junior S.O.S. after several days and hours of workshops for its members that take place usually on Saturday afternoon and Saturday night. Contests afford the juniors chances to compete. Sponsors provide prize money for dance competitions at the National Shag Dance Championship held in March at Myrtle

Beach and the Grand Nationals Dance Championship in Atlanta. The fun, camaraderie, and competition help cement young shaggers' love for the dance. Junior shaggers are taking their place in the shag culture as future ambassadors of the dance, as their association motto states: "The future of shag dancing lies in the hearts and feet of our juniors."

Back in the legendary days of O.D., youngsters flocked to the beach and learned to dance by watching others and dancing. With the glory days of the beach bums and "on the beach" in the past, many young people today learn from instructors. They attend S.O.S. functions and events and meet other young shaggers who will become Keepers of the Dance, an organization recognizing those who began as junior shaggers and who as adults continue to promote the shag.

Keepers of the Dance inducts junior shaggers who continue to dance competitively and socially after reaching the age of twenty-one. Annually two young people under the age of forty are inducted into the Keepers of the Dance Hall of Fame during ShagAttack, the same event where the Shag Hall of Fame recognizes eight new inductees each year.

Such events are fun too. At Highlight for the Heart—Jr. S.O.S. 2010, juniors learned to shag in a family atmosphere and then roasted marshmallows at a bonfire on the beach. Good values prevail. The 2010 Jr. S.O.S. concluded on a Sunday with breakfast at Fat Harold's followed by a devotional hour. The emphasis on good behavior runs counterpoint to how things were in the glory years. Chief Bellamy, the Wizard, would be pleased.

An educational emphasis exists as well. The Shad Alberty Scholarship awards one thousand dollars each year to a high school senior or college student. Each applicant must write an essay on a subject that event directors choose. The Beth Mitchell Memorial Scholarship and Dewey Kennedy Scholarship further junior shaggers' education as well.

The Ellen Taylor Foundation for Junior Shaggers, a nonprofit charitable foundation, dedicates its efforts to providing financial assistance in the education, preservation, and promotion of the shag, South Carolina's state dance. Taylor, a Winnsboro, South Carolina, native, founded the organization in 2007 to help families of juniors overcome financial barriers that prevent those under twenty-one from learning and participating in the shag. She credits Donna and Rusty Hosaflook for the idea and for encouraging her to establish the Ellen Taylor Foundation for Junior Shaggers.

The foundation donates free dance shoes, which are good, conditioned shoes recycled from the shag community. For qualifying families, the foundation also funds workshops and provides meals, lodging, and gas vouchers for shag dance events such as Junior S.O.S. at North Myrtle Beach.

There's a saying that people perpetuate those things they love. From the past comes Taylor's motivation for promoting the shag and helping assure its future. Her passion for teaching and helping teens to dance began as many good things do—in a less-than-cheery childhood.

"The earlier years of my childhood weren't the happiest experience," explained Taylor. "My mom and dad divorced when I was seven years of age and because mom couldn't work and take care of us, my brothers and I were taken care of by relatives."

Her mother did shift work at the local cotton mill, and Taylor and her brothers saw very little of her during that period. In time their mother married Grover "Pop" Drawdy, who was the recreation director at the community recreation center in Winnsboro and also the recreation director for the state of South Carolina. Therein lay a connection to one of shag's iconic figures and quite a coincidence. "Pop and Billy Jeffers, director of Recreation in Florence, South Carolina, were the best of friends," said Taylor. And then, in one of those shag moments, two future Hall of Famers met.

"It was at a meeting in Florence as a teenager when I met him," said Taylor. Jeffers was one of the first to be inducted into the Shaggers Hall of Fame in 1983. "How unbelievable is it that three years after his induction into this prestigious organization I, too, had the honor of being inducted?" Taylor asked.

Her childhood set her on track to become a Hall of Famer and an influence on young shaggers. "Mom continued to work shift work at the U.S. Rubber Company in Winnsboro after she and Pop married," said Taylor, "so my afternoons after school were spent at the recreation center." There she participated in all the sports activities, but her favorite thing to do was hang around the jukebox and watch teenagers dance. She remembered, "I loved this part of each day and looked forward to school being out and getting to the center because occasionally the guys would take the time to dance with me. When I would get home from an afternoon of dancing with the older guys, I would go into the bedroom, hold on to the bedpost, and pretend to be dancing with one of the guys."

Taylor remembers too how she was introduced to the dance at the beach during family and business trips: "Once I reached my teen years, while our parents were busy with their meetings and dinner parties, we teenagers began to venture out to the local places to watch the dancing."

THE JO JO MOJO

One of shag's enduring legends, Jo Jo Putnam danced the shag in its glory days, Dark Ages, and comeback years. A crowd pleaser, he dances here with Judy Drake.

Photograph courtesy of Phil Sawyer.

One day at the Myrtle Beach Pavilion by the jukebox near the flagpole, a noisy throng of people attracted her and her friends. They were watching a couple dancing. The man dancing impressed Taylor, as he would many others.

Spectators told her that the guy's name was Jo Jo. The impression stuck, and that, combined with her childhood memories, set the stage for a chance to help other teens down the road. Once again shagging fate would intervened in 1990, when Putnam and Taylor would grace *Sandlapper* magazine's cover.

"Those years growing up at the 'Y' as we called the recreation center, and having the opportunity to watch dancers at the Pavilion, later in my teen years while on vacations at Ocean Drive watching the dancers at the pavilion, I knew I had to dance. It was my way of expressing all the emotions I had experienced in my life and is still the way I dance today—from the heart," Taylor said. Today one of her life joys, a matter close to her heart, is working with young people. As she explained, "Through the years, I have watched many of our young people grow from their beginning moments as a junior shagger [*sic*] into adulthood."

Taylor and other shaggers realize that recruiting young people to the dance assures that the shag culture can dance into the future. Junior shaggers feed the shag river a tributary of youth.

The need to keep the dance going through young people isn't lost on Mike Marr. In "Keeping the Dance Alive," Marr wrote: "Spring is the time for young ideas, young music, and young people. . . . The purpose of S.O.S. is to keep the dance alive and the best way to do that is to bring in new dancers. Youth and shag go together like Weejuns and hardwood floors."

Ellen Taylor would agree that they indeed go together. In addition they go a long way toward ensuring the shag's future *and* its dancers' deftness.

"Let me say that the future of our dance is in very good hands," Taylor stated. Referring to 2009, she said, "Last year we had over 600 in attendance at Junior S.O.S. for the shag workshops. It is awesome to watch them progress in their ability from one workshop to the next, from one day to the next, from one week to the next, from one year to the next. Those juniors who began only a few years ago are taking this dance to a new level, and I feel with each new generation the dance will change and get even better than it is today."

CLUBS SPREAD SHAG FEVER

The Association of Carolina Shag Clubs helps groups establish shag clubs that spread the dance to new locales. A lot of shag territory has been covered since the Columbia Shag Club became the first shag club in February 1982. The original shag club's official motto is "It's a good day to play," and ninety-seven clubs later that playful shag spirit keeps spreading.

Today close to one hundred clubs introduce the shag to newcomers. Shag clubs have spread from the beach into areas such as Chattanooga and Pittsburgh, the "Steel City." Quite by chance a fellow from Pittsburgh was vacationing in Myrtle Beach in the early 1980s. He wandered up to Ocean Drive during an early S.O.S. event and couldn't believe what he saw.

Burning with shag fever, he returned to Pittsburgh. A few months later he brought a busload of eager Steelers to the beach. They came; they saw; they caught the fever. Today the Steel City Boogie Club exists, thanks to one man who wandered up to Ocean Drive and was smitten by beach fever and the shag.

As for Chattanooga, that city in the shadow of Lookout Mountain, a career transfer took one longtime shagger, teacher, and club officer to Chattanooga. There he started a shag club.

Curiosity, career moves, and more have let the shag hitch a ride and spread beyond its North and South Carolina origins. An alphabetical list shows ninety-eight shag clubs that stretch from Aiken to York, South Carolina. But don't let the first and twenty-fifth letters fool you. In between A and Y you'll find cities with shag clubs all over the alphabet. The only letters without shag clubs are I, Q, V, and Z. Can the shag spread to Idaho Falls, Idaho; Quincy, Massachusetts; Victoria, Texas; or Zephyrhills, Florida? Why not? Just give the shag a little more time.

Yesteryear's cool, smooth dance ambassadors in their drapes and cashmere sweaters would be surprised to see that their dance has clubs in places well beyond the Carolinas. West Virginians have long traveled to the Grand Strand to vacation, and many West Virginians took the shag back to the mountains. Charleston, West Virginia, has the Almost Heaven WV Shaggers, and South Charleston, Beckley, Bluefield, and Parkersburg have clubs too. Irondale, Alabama, has the Beach Shaggers of Birmingham. Tennessee and Virginia have clubs. Tampa, Florida, has the Sun Coast Shag Club and the Tampa Bay Beach Boppers. By far the most clubs are in North and South Carolina, but the dance and its cult continue to spread.

Some club names are as colorful as shaggers' nicknames from the glory days. Some names betray their locations far from the beach: Almost Heaven Shag Club; Battlefield Boogie Shag Club; Brushy Mountain Shag Club; Choo Choo Shag Club; Electric City Shag Club; Mid Ohio Valley Shaggers Inc.; Music City Bop Club; Pittsburgh Area Jitterbug Club; Roanoke Valley Shag Club; ShagAtlanta (spelled Internet style); Smoky Mountain Shaggers; Steel City Boogie Club; and others.

Other clubs subscribe to the ACSC. Though not full association members, these clubs spread the shag culture too. A few club names indicate how the shag has danced its way into new territory far from Ocean Drive and Carolina Beach: Beach Boppers of Orlando; Cincinnati Bop Club; Daytona Beach Club; Derby City Bop Assn. Inc. (Louisville, Kentucky); Mid-Ohio Boogie Club (New Albany, Ohio); Seven Hills Shaggers (Rome, Georgia).

Fully affiliated clubs comprise the Association of Shag Clubs, conceived back when Ron Whisenant of Rock Hill and Phil Sawyer of Columbia met during shag's great revival. Today the Association of Carolina Shag Clubs Inc., known as ACSC, provides communications among the clubs, coordinates club activities, and sponsors activities of mutual interest to all clubs. In addition it manages and operates the Society of Stranders. The association promotes and preserves the heritage of beach music and shag dancing. The clubs plan many events, and the association helps clubs avoid schedule conflicts. As well it awards the ACSC Shagging Icon award to individuals who make outstanding contributions within their local full-member shag clubs and are exemplary shag community members.

Jan Weakley (2003 Icon) and Sharon Jones (2001 Icon) played key roles in the enhancement of the awards and their selection process. Jones, a member of the Outer Banks Shag Club, and Weakley, a member of the Virginia Beach Shag Club, cochaired the Icon Enhancement Committee in 2005 to improve the Icon awards. Previously the ACSC and S.O.S. boards administered the awards. Weakley said that though some nominees may be well known in the shag world, many individuals might not be known outside their own clubs.

Weakley and Jones cochair the Icon Selection Committee. Nominations must come from the current president, vice president, or past president of a full-member ACSC club. The Icon award represents one of the most cherished prizes a shagger can attain, and its granting is based on years in a club, offices held, committees chaired and served, participation in major events, and the promotion of the shag and S.O.S., as well as other factors. The Icon Selection Committee consists of volunteers from past winners. At this writing eighty-two Icons have been inducted since the award's inception in 1995.

SHAG'S TORCHBEARERS

Other agents spreading the shag? Dance instructors. Consider Johanna and John Hall's "Miss Grace." It evokes images of a dance floor where friends and lovers move to eight beats in two bars of music. The steps may seem simple. The truth is, they aren't. And yet a new learner can shag even with a door.

Many a beginner has learned the basic step while hanging on to a doorknob. With the basic in their repertoire, into the shag world they go. And once out in the world of shag? Well, the possibilities are endless. Now experience becomes the master teacher. Along with improvisations come moments to remember, new friends, and perhaps romance.

Today a lot of newcomers learn to shag thanks to instructors. Of the shag, a Georgia humorist, the late Lewis Grizzard, said, "The shag is like doing the jitterbug on Valium." He was alluding to its slowed-down, silken moves.

If anyone understands how to execute those silken moves, shag instructors do. Thumb through an S.O.S. *Carefree Times* and you'll find ad headlines for shag instructors: Sam and Lisa West Workshops; Charlie Womble and Jackie McGee; DanceLink USA Studio; and Shag Workshops with Ellen Taylor, for example. A search on the Internet reveals more instructors than can be listed here.

Michael Norris and LeAnn Best Norris have taught the shag all over the country to people of all walks of life. "Once people learn the dance it gets in their soul and they are hooked. They will then tell a friend and it spreads like wild fire. All it takes is one trip to dance class or S.O.S. and people cannot believe how much fun it can be," they explained.

Having some instruction isn't a bad thing. The dance and its music have evolved. *Livin' Out Loud* magazine (with permission from Nancy Hall Publications) discussed the shag's fundamental step and some of its moves: "The dance has evolved over the years to have a myriad of variations, but all begin with a basic step that works well with a 4/4 rhythmic structure. Steps include classic moves called Start, Turns, and mirror moves such as the Pivot, and moves like the Belly Roll, Boogie Walk, Kickback with Lean, Pause, Side Step, Prissy and Sugarfoot."

But what if you can't shag, much less execute the classic moves? What if you're attracted to the shag and just want to be a solid dancer and not worry about contests—in other words just become a "good" shagger?

Taylor offers some advice: "To become the best social dancer you can be, no doubt, you have to have a good, solid foundation in the fundamentals. Until you can get on the floor with a partner, dance without having to count the steps, and learn to be a good follower/leader, you will not be the dancer you are looking to be. (This, of course, is for those who have never shagged and learned by instruction.)"

Taylor serves up a dance approach: "My theory since becoming an instructor is to learn with the head, dance with the heart, interpret with the feet. It is a question/answer—action/reaction. Your partner speaks, you answer. One rule I have for my students is to never 'out dance' your partner. Dance on the level of that person you are dancing with even if they do nothing but the very basic steps. This is a lead-follow dance and you have to learn to be a good leader in order to let your dance partner know where you want her to go. The guys are the leaders. 'Lead me and I will follow you.' A good follower will not go anywhere the guy doesn't lead her unless she has the ability to read subtle turns of the wrist or hand and moves accordingly, but this is rare and isn't something you can teach."

The accomplished dancers who have mastered shag's intricacies put on quite a show, and it can prove quite surprising how light big men can be on their feet. This proves that the potential for dancers isn't limited to people of certain dimensions: the shag appeals to people of all sizes, and therein is one reason the dance keeps attracting its devotees.

Those devotees fit no one stereotypical perception. Charley Holtzclaw grew up in Kannapolis. There, he said, he "was privileged to witness some great shaggers. A. V. Franklin, Henry Eller, Mike Osbourne, and Glynn Compton, to name a few. Glynn weighed well over 300 lbs, but was as light as a feather on his feet. Girls lined up to dance with him."

The late Shad Alberty, a showstopper of a dancer, played a role in the shag's revival in the late 1960s and early 1970s. His name was long synonymous with shag contests throughout North and South Carolina. He promoted contests, and some believe he may have taught more students than anyone else. He even taught Academy Award winner Robert Duvall when Duvall was appearing in the shooting of *Days of Thunder* in Darlington, South Carolina, in 1990. After a day's shooting Duvall would ease over to a little shag bar in Florence every night to shag. He too perhaps became a shag ambassador.

Learning to shag is life-changing for some. Take Michael Norris, for example, who said, "A one-hour dance class in 1990 changed my life forever. I met my wife, paid for college, met my best friend, and now run The USA Grand National Dance Championships—all because I took a shag class. My wife, LeAnn, and I feel teaching others to dance is more than just a dance lesson. It keeps the dance alive." On May 30, 2010, Charlie Womble and Jackie McGee passed the Grand Nationals torch to Michael and LeAnn Norris.

Shag's instructors take pride in their role as dance ambassadors. Susie Beaver of High Point, North Carolina, teaches the shag. She owns and directs the Susie Beaver Dance Company, and her résumé reads like a shag dance honor roll with multiple national shag champions and service as a judge of competitions.

"How exciting for all of us who teach the dance," said Beaver. "Our dance and our music have become very, very popular both nationally and internationally, due to the efforts and hard work by many of us professional teachers, who travel throughout our country and the world teaching and sharing our dance." Beaver, who has been teaching the shag for thirty-five years and is a full-time Master-Professional Carolina shag teacher/coach, continued: "My passion for teaching is like no other." Her life illustrates something you hear time and time again: "The shag is not just a dance; it's a lifestyle!"

As new people take up the shag, change is inevitable and at times unwelcome. Dance instructors Michael and LeAnn Best Norris have a message for all shaggers: "We need to spread this dance to keep it alive. Get the young people involved and be open to change. Things cannot stay the same way they were 50 years ago. Don't categorize a dancer just because of the shoes he/she is wearing. The shoes do not make the dancer[;] the soul does. The main thing is they are shagging."

Of course it wasn't always this way. Laughter in 2011 reminisced, saying that in the beginning no one taught the shag. "Very few good dancers existed," he said.

DANCE CONTESTS PULL THEM IN

Back in 1973's dark-age summer, a dance contest at the Jolly Knave gave the shag a shot in the arm. The contests pulled in droves of shag fans. The desire to dance at higher levels was still alive too. Individuals and couples consistently winning contests found a market: would-be dancers eager to learn and good dancers who yearned to be great dancers.

In 1981 the S.O.S. promoted a shag contest with five thousand dollars in prize money. A flyer ran a headline, "Any Excuse for a Party." It was a two-night soirée held on May 29 and May 30 at Columbia's Jamil Temple. Two dance floors were reserved, with one being held for the competitors. Among the judges was one Leon Williams. The building's capacity was three thousand, and the contest was hyped as maybe the biggest inland beach party ever staged.

Though popular, contests proved contentious in the early days. The 1984 S.O.S. Migration program carried a front-page disclaimer: "Any shag contest that may take place during the S.O.S. Migration is NOT sponsored by the S.O.S. and is NOT a part of the S.O.S. PROGRAM. The purpose of S.O.S. Migration is for EVERYONE to have fun."

In the winter 1985 newsletter Laughter responded to a letter requesting that S.O.S. hold dance contests, writing, "We held one in Nome, Alaska, in 1983. It was won by Charlie Porter and Paula, the dancing bear. The S.O.S. plans a highland fling in '87 to be held at a loch on Scotland. Big prizes. Details later."

In a 1985 *Carefree Times* newsletter, one letter to the editor stood up for the dance contests. It read: "I read your sarcastic reply to the letter requesting an S.O.S. shag contest. It wasn't funny. If S.O.S. doesn't schedule a contest soon, I don't plan to renew."

Laughter's response? "Why wait? Enclosed is a full refund for this year's membership. You are out scot-free. Bye!"

The S.O.S. had started out as a group whose goal was just to have fun. As it grew, it changed, and dance contests fueled dissent. A woman from Greenville, South Carolina, wrote about how things were changing: "So much has changed within this shaggers' group since 1980. What started out as a reunion for all beach and shag lovers has turned into numerous areas of classification: Hall of Famers, novices, professional contenders, professionals, etc. Who decided where we all belong? I, for one, wish we could have remained one—a group of overgrown kids longing to be with their own—no competition, no classification."

An organization was formed to calm the troubled waters. The Shaggers Preservation Association (SPA) emerged from a meeting at the Internationale Hotel in North Myrtle Beach in November 1981 to oversee shag contests.

According to the SPA's history on its Web site, "The idea of an organization of Beach Clubs in the Carolinas was born out of what was considered to be a necessity by some club owners. Shag contests were very popular at this time but there were many problems. These problems centered around competition for dancers between true beach clubs and other businesses, formats for holding contests, standards for judging and many more. Born out of controversy, this idea was to suffer many more trying times, heated discussions and even a few fisticuffs."

Things settled down, and today the SPA, a nonprofit organization registered in North and South Carolina, promotes and preserves the shag. Sanctioned and nonsanctioned dance contests continue to spread the shag, though some purists frown on contests, believing they run against the grain of the old days when shaggers pioneered their moves as they danced.

Differences of opinion aside, accomplished dancers and contests attract to the shag people who are unaware of the shag's illustrious history.

Charlie Womble and Jackie McGee (Womble) are consummate shaggers. Their accolades pile up like sand dunes. In an occurrence of manifest dance

CHARLIE WOMBLE AND JACKIE MCGEE

Shag's winning form, demonstrated here by nine-time National Shag
Champions, U.S. Open Swing Champions, Shaggers Hall of Fame, Shad Alberty
Award recipients, Three-Time Feather Award winners for Best Male and Female
Swing Dancers, Best Classic Swing winning couple, and New Wave Award
winners. They long produced the Grand National Dance Championship.

Photograph courtesy of Phil Sawyer.

destiny, they helped the shag reach the West Coast. In 1989 the Wombles introduced the Carolina shag to the U.S. Open in Los Angeles. West Coast swingers and southern shaggers connected. The first shag instructors the S.O.S. endorsed, they too have spread the dance.

Contests serve as social functions that stoke dancers' competitive spirit. Curious onlookers come to see the winners and enjoy the music and dance moves. Michael and LeAnn Norris believe contests force dancers to practice and create new shag moves and leads. "Over the years I have taken non-dancing friends to shag contests, and when we leave there they are amazed," said Michael. "Several began lessons as a result of attending the contest. Plus competition has a slight bit more 'flair' and is a little more attractive to a 'non-dancer' as well."

The Norrises said that many of their friends look at the shag culture in many ways: "We have friends who look at it as going to the beach and hanging out and drinking a beer and dancing. Others look at it as a sport. They take lessons, practice, and compete. Both ways are great."

Not all like the contest aspect of the shag. Some go as far as to say it hurts the classic shag by placing too much emphasis on fancy footwork. The summer 1983 *S.O.S. News,* forerunner to *Carefree Times,* ran a notice that the September 15, 1983, *Sand Flea Beach* also ran, a tongue-in-cheek ad promoting a "Million Dollar S.O.S. Championship Invitational Shag Contest."

The copy proclaimed, "The largest, most glamorous shag contest in history is coming up. It's the first (and last) S.O.S. $1,000,000 invitational to be held in Nome, Alaska on December 25 at the Igloo Beach Club. Two divisions: clones and Pro-Clones." The "ad" went on, announcing (in all caps), "Reservations for the black-tie, foot-long hot dog dinner can be made through your travel agent. Soon to be a major motion picture." In an interesting aside, just beneath the so-called ad was a legitimate ad from the Tams thanking their fans, DJs, and record shops for standing by them for the past twenty years: "We all love you! —The Tams."

BEYOND TOMORROW

About the time the dark ages had the shag in a cold, dry grip, Sonny Bono wrote "The Beat Goes On," a song that peaked on the charts on January 14, 1967. Some of the lyrics fit the shag's pedigree and shaggers, such as the Charleston, the beat going on, and kissing, for instance. However, no S.O.S. grandmothers sit in armchairs and reminisce. Nor do grandfathers. As was the case for the juniors and the fellow from Pittsburgh, the ripple touched them all.

BRENDA AND MIKE PACE

Hall of Fame Shaggers go through the paces. Though shagging
is a basic set of steps, no two people dance the same way.

Photograph courtesy of Phil Sawyer.

Like a stone thrown into a pond, the shag keeps rippling outward from its legendary beginnings. For every town it passes through, for every person it touches, for every club it fills, it brings a zest for life, letting many recapture their youth. For newcomers, it gives them a way to be happy and forget their worries for a while. Feeling good and having fun prove contagious—always have and always will—and they spread the shag and its good-time culture.

Joan Kimbro expressed a sentiment that many shaggers share when it comes to the shag and the fun and camaraderie the S.O.S., for want of a better term, "institutionalized": "It has grown beyond anyone's imagination and now I am seeing people from all walks of life picking up where they left off as kids. Kind of like riding a bicycle, it does come back. Once you take that first step, it is like a shot of youth. You are somehow taken back to being that kid again and your feet don't care if your face has wrinkles or you have a potbelly. You soon realize all the stress you packed up and brought to the beach is gone. You are free and you are happy and you can't wait until the next event. As an older gentleman told me one night at the Arcade, this sure beats a nursing home and I feel alive again."

Kimbro continued: "Maybe people who are lonely and miserable will read this book and realize they can break free of this pit and find the person hiding inside. Shaggers are happy people. There is no age barrier; on the dance floor we are all equal. Shaggers also love to share their steps, so if you need a little help, a total stranger will offer to help. Shagging is also a basic set of steps but no two people do the same thing. Each person is allowed to bring his or her personality into this dance. I have always told couples to dance as they feel comfortable. This is your time so make it fun and dance till you feel all that newfound energy. The most rewarding thing I have realized through shagging is the ability to meet people from almost everywhere." Kimbro expressed just why the shag has spread and why it is moving into the future giving generations to come the opportunity to experience the joy shaggers have known since the late 1940s: "a shot of youth."

State of South Carolina
Proclamation
by
Governor Jim Hodges

WHEREAS, with a long and proud tradition of local artists and a growing population of beach music fans spanning across generations, South Carolina has designated beach music as the official popular music of the Palmetto State; and

WHEREAS, over the past 50 years, the development of beach music has contributed tremendously to the enjoyment of the citizens of our state, with the South Carolina General Assembly designating the Shag as the official Dance of the Palmetto State in 1984; and

WHEREAS, each year, residents and visitors alike visit the South Carolina coast to enjoy the sounds of beach music, while participating in dance competitions and festivals that offer fun for the entire family; and

WHEREAS, as beach music has continued to grow and spread into national prominence, South Carolina has emerged as a leader in the development of this unique art form.

NOW, THEREFORE, I, Jim Hodges, Governor of the Great State of South Carolina, do hereby proclaim April 18, 2001, as

BEACH MUSIC DAY

throughout the state and encourage all South Carolinians to recognize the positive impact of beach music on the enjoyment and cultural development of the citizens of the Palmetto State.

Jim Hodges
Governor
State of South Carolina

BEACH MUSIC DAY

Governor Jim Hodges designated April 18, 2001, as Beach Music Day, not to be confused with Act No, 329, 1984 that designated the shag as the "official dance of the State."

Courtesy of Phil Sawyer.

Appendix A

Shagonomics

In the beginning shaggers had little money, and what money they had went to the jukebox, beer, and hotdogs. Of course they had those tailored drapes and cashmere sweaters, but those were acquired at great sacrifice. In addition they would toss pennies at rookie dancers who violated dance protocol. Well, that was then; this is now, and Father Time has sure changed their economic circumstances.

The beach bums are bums no longer. The days when shaggers were lucky to have loose change in their pockets are long gone. Growing up and building careers put shaggers on more solid financial footing, and today they represent careers of all kinds. "We have doctors, lawyers, congressmen, auto mechanics, factory workers," said Ron Whisenant, S.O.S. president, in a September interview with Johanna D. Wilson, writer with *TheSunNews.com*. "The people are from all walks of life," he reported. Today's S.O.S. dancers don't toss pennies; they support many good causes.

At this writing, a fee of thirty-five dollars a year gets a membership in the S.O.S. from January 1 to December 31. The dues carry a subscription to *Carefree Times* magazine, "the Shagger's *Bible,*" which provides information on recent events, activities, upcoming events, local shag clubs, shag merchandise, and other shag-related items of interest. The dues provide unlimited access (no cover charge) to participating lounges for the duration of both ten-day S.O.S. events and the three-day Mid-Winter Break, which are close to the hearts of shaggers. Dues also provide discounts at many shops and restaurants, but these pale in comparison to other expenditures.

Shaggers spend a lot of money going to and from dance venues. Travel, lodging, gas, food, drinks—the list goes on. They contribute to the economy, educational institutions, and a variety of good causes. To have started out as a bunch of beach bums, members of the S.O.S and ACSC do all right. They even have their own corporate flowchart.

In addition, like any well-oiled financial machine, the S.O.S. has corporate sponsors. For $1,000 a year a merchant or business can be a Platinum sponsor. A Gold sponsorship runs $500 a year, and a Silver sponsorship for shag stakeholders runs $250. Yes, the beach bums have turned corporate.

THE TIMES THEY DO CHANGE

Once told not to come back to O.D., shaggers have long been welcome. A May 14, 1990, column in the *Sun News* referred to a South Carolina Parks, Recreation, and Tourism study provided by the S.O.S. revealing that the S.O.S. "pumps $5 million into the North Myrtle beach economy [the $5 million was an error, $10 million was the correct figure]."

Some thirty years later the shag's economic boost has changed things bigtime for a group of bums once considered undesirables. Can you imagine the penny-tossing, beer-guzzling dancers being members of a conventional organization such as a chamber of commerce? Well, some of them are.

"Money changes everything" per the 1984 eponymous song. In 1987 S.O.S. joined the North Myrtle Beach Chamber of Commerce. Wrote Laughter, "Yep, this is the same group that wouldn't give me the time of day when S.O.S. was just a germ of an idea."

The matured shag culture's ability to draw people to the beach provided a much-appreciated boon to the beach economy. In 1987 the *Sand Flea* quoted Laughter on how the S.O.S. attracted a crowd: "We've got members from 29 states that come back for this gathering. It's one hell of a boost for the local North Myrtle Beach economy." One hell of a boost is right.

As the years have passed, the S.O.S. has both grown and found new ways to increase its revenue. It has legally protected its logo and licensed its use on shirts, jewelry, tapes, towels, and books, all of which brought in new earnings for the S.O.S. and the association. A partying group of adults isn't shy about spending money, and a lot of that money goes into the North Myrtle Beach economy.

"Shagonomics" is about numbers. The Association of Carolina Shag Clubs has 98 full-member clubs with a total membership of 15,436. There are also 28 subscriber members such as lounges, dance schools, record stores, and others.

The S.O.S. had just over 12,000 members in 2008 when estimates projected that more than 15,000 attended the fall and spring events. The estimate for the mid-winter event stood at 10,000. The power of numbers leads to the power of giving. With more than a few pennies in its pockets, the S.O.S. continues to be generous.

A HISTORY OF GIVING

Not only can shaggers cut a rug; they can also cut a check. In 1981 the "beach bums," as they call themselves, revealed their charitable side early on. An S.O.S. newsletter feature, "S.O.S. Beachcombings," publicized plans to "help build the North Myrtle Beach library." The S.O.S. contributed profits to the North Myrtle Beach Friends of the Library.

In 1989 the Association of Carolina Shag Clubs and S.O.S. contributed ten thousand dollars to the American Red Cross for Hurricane Hugo relief. Shaggers' reverence for the coast of North and South Carolina motivated them to donate funds to the Red Cross to replenish spent funds and to provide additional relief. Around that time the S.O.S. donated one thousand dollars to the city of North Myrtle Beach to help maintain and landscape the monument that honors the contributions dancers have made to the city throughout the decades.

The September 23–29, 2010, issue of the *North Myrtle Beach Times* published a front-page feature, "S.O.S. Fall Migration Ends Sunday." In the report was yet another indication of how the love for beach music and the shag provides charitable benefits. It read: "Last year the shaggers donated $19,340 to the American Red Cross in North Myrtle Beach to benefit victims of the fire." An April 2009 wildfire destroyed approximately seventy homes and charred more than 30 square miles. This year they hope to earn more money for local charities."

While the larger shag organizations contribute to charities, associated organizations and individual clubs adopt their own charities and causes. The following paragraphs describe but a few clubs and the charitable contributions they make.

The Northern Virginia Shag Club's chosen charity is Capital Hospice. Club member and onetime officer Heather Jennings had an idea to raise money for hospice. Her idea came to fruition, and the "Shag-a-thon" was born. It became a labor of love for the club. In July 2010 the club presented Capital Hospice a check for $191,000.

The Beaufort Shag Club annually sponsors "Boogie for the Boys," a charitable effort that helps boys ages fourteen to seventeen who have been referred by the juvenile justice system or have failed in traditional school settings. The recipient of the charity, AMIKids Beaufort, provides a second chance for young men who otherwise would be sent to jail for their nonviolent offenses. This nonprofit residential program for at-risk boys has served more than 1,780 youths since opening its doors in 1985. AMIKids operates fifty-six programs in eight states, including the Beaufort program in South Carolina, one of its most successful programs.

The O.D. Shag Club gave four thousand dollars to Camp Kemo in 2010. As well it donated to such diverse charities as the Junior Shag Association, the North Myrtle Beach Humane Society, Citizens Against Spousal Abuse, Helping Hands, Mobile Meals for the homebound, and Teen Angels, which helps homeless teenagers. The club donated two thousand dollars to the North Myrtle Beach Police Department, whose "Shop with a Cop" program puts joy in the lives of children who are underprivileged and have special needs. The police take the children shopping the week before Christmas and treat them to lunch.

The Hall of Fame Foundation was established in 1991 to provide financial aid to shaggers of all ages and circumstances. Its motto is "A History of Friends Caring for Friends." Its grants are based only on financial need, regardless of race, religion, dance ability, or any other criteria. The Hall of Fame Foundation is not affiliated with the Shagger's Hall of Fame. It is an eleemosynary organization in South Carolina with IRS 501(3)(c) tax-exempt status. Foundation contributions traditionally come from shaggers and shag-affiliated organizations.

Another charitable organization is the Ellen Taylor Foundation for Junior Shaggers, mentioned in chapter 11. Its purpose is to remove the financial barriers that prevent kids from learning the shag and from participating in shag dance events. The ETFJS is a 501(3)(c) corporation. The foundation's Junior S.O.S. Shoe Program distributes free dance shoes to junior shaggers.

The S.O.S. contributes to Camp Kemo. Camp Kemo provides a special summer week for children with cancer and their siblings. Sharing this experience with children with the same concerns gives them strength and support and helps increase their self-esteem so they can better reenter mainstream life.

UNIVERSITY OF SOUTH CAROLINA
SCHOOL OF DANCE ENDOWMENT

Funds raised by the S.O.S. go to many good causes, among them a dance endowment. An article that first appeared in the *Columbia Star,* and also appeared on the University of South Carolina College of Arts and Sciences Theatre and Dance Web site, gives in part an account of how this endowment came to pass: "Membership in S.O.S. is the ticket to take the floor during two seasonal events that for more than two decades have drawn shaggers to the Carolina coast. Today, S.O.S. has a membership of approximately 18,000 Carolina Shag lovers worldwide, although most dancers are located primarily in the Southeast. Spring Safari, considered a baby-boomers' Spring Break, attracts as many as 15,000 dancers to the North Myrtle Beach area. Fall Migration brings in about the same number, turning participating shag halls, decks, or boardwalks into tourist destinations."

It wasn't always this way, as we know by now. Among those keeping the dance alive is Phil Sawyer. The S.O.S. honored Sawyer for his role in getting the shag back on its dance feet. "The honor carries with it the establishment of the Phil Sawyer Award, an annual cash award intended as a partial scholarship for a dance major in the University of South Carolina's Department of Theatre and Dance."

Two gifts to the Dr. Phil Huff Sawyer Scholarship, a five-thousand-dollar one from the ACSC and twenty thousand dollars from the S.O.S. Charitable Foundation, established the fund. Annual income to the S.O.S. funded the award, and it quickly exceeded its one-hundred-thousand-dollar goal to become a named scholarship in perpetuity. The University of South Carolina Department of Theatre and Dance administers the scholarship. The endowment enables students to earn bachelor of arts degrees in dance education.

In the early 1990s the Association of Carolina Shag Clubs donated one hundred thousand dollars to the Foundation of the Carolinas, a 501(c)(3) charitable organization that was established with the assistance of Duke University. All profits generated by the one hundred thousand dollars go to the National Association of Hospice.

S.O.S. has proven to be an intuitive fund-raiser and a shrewd event organizer. When it expanded its annual Fall Migration to North Myrtle Beach to ten days, a problem surfaced. A lot of shaggers would go home for a few days right after the first weekend. The solution was Fun Sunday and Fun Monday, events overseen by the ad hoc Enhancement Committee. Hollis Britt, who chairs this committee, said that the committee was formed to help the S.O.S. and area merchants. They use local vendors, and the theme remains constant: partying and fun.

On the first Sunday and only Monday of the Fall Migration shaggers meet in North Myrtle Beach for two huge block parties. Fun Sunday is a street party alongside Elaine Hunter's OD Arcade, a club that mirrors S.O.S.'s growth. The spillover from Duck's and Harold's first filled her small arcade, a place with skee ball, a pinball machine, and a tiny bar. She moved the pool tables and put a small wooden floor in place and added a deejay booth. Her place grew, and Elaine, an easygoing lady who runs a tight ship, watched her arcade become one of the Stranders' more popular hot spots. Porch parties on Saturdays with deejay Murl Augustine pack in people wearing T-shirts proclaiming, "We're Porch People."

Some of the best names in beach and shag music play at Fun Sunday as thousands dance and extend their money's stay through the weekend into the week. Fun Monday packs shaggers in from Main Street to Hillside. There's dancing in the street, and local vendors and S.O.S. sponsors set up shop.

Fun Monday provides funding for the S.O.S. Charitable Foundation through a raffle. Any proceeds that remain after Fun Monday expenses are paid go to charity. Both the S.O.S. Charitable Fund and Caring 4 Kids of Horry County, for instance, benefit from the Fun Monday raffle. The lucky holders of winning tickets go home with some money, and those buying the tickets know they're helping people in need.

The Spring Migration, not to be outdone, features its Saturday parade, chaired for more than fifteen years by Don David. On the last Saturday of Spring S.O.S everyone meets on Main Street for the ACSC Club's parade, another economic stimulus for the area. Clubs turn to float rental companies and various costume providers among other businesses to outfit their colorful, often zany floats.

ACSC member clubs plan, design, and build parade floats for fun and a chance to win one of the coveted awards in the categories for best shag theme, most original float, shagging troop, and best club vehicle. The Spring Safari parade always draws a huge crowd that finds a lot of ways to let go of money.

The S.O.S. established the S.O.S. Charitable Foundation as a means of contributing to other charitable foundations. Total donations from the S.O.S. Charitable Foundation to charities generally exceed $30,000 each year, though 2010's amount was $24,000. In 2007, $36,400 was donated to charities. The S.O.S. and the S.O.S. Charitable Foundation, it should be noted, operate independently of one another.

All this generosity and good fortune sprang from a little dance that folks fell in love with long ago along the Atlantic Seaboard. The years rolled by bringing prosperity and inviting interest. The money generated by S.O.S. activities along the coast in Ocean Drive invited research, and the resulting figures from a Coastal Carolina University study, though not an in-depth study, reveal how annual shag events stimulate the economy in the North Myrtle Beach region.

SHAGONOMIC'S ANALYSIS
AND ECONOMIC IMPACT

At the request of the S.O.S., the Coastal Federal Center for Economic and Community Development of Coastal Carolina University conducted an analysis and economic impact study of the 2004 Fall Migration. The study centered on ten questions that 525 Migration participants answered. The questions sought information on visitors by states, distance traveled, spending per visitor, accommodations, length of stay, activities, and the likelihood that they would attend future S.O.S. events, among other items of economic interest.

The study was conducted under the auspices of the Coastal Federal Center for Economic and Community Development and the E. Craig Wall Sr. College of Business Administration. The study's principal investigator was Yoav Wachsman, assistant professor of economics at Coastal Carolina University.

Results revealed that more people are likely to come to North Myrtle Beach during migrations than other times, an obvious finding considering the timing of such events. The S.O.S. plans its Migrations to the beach at times when the usual beach throngs are elsewhere. S.O.S. events avoid those times when crowds of Canadians, students, and bikers flock to the Grand Strand. As a result S.O.S. events provide economic stimulus during nontraditional "beach" times.

The study's introduction referred to the ten-day "adult parties." These "adult parties have a strong, economic impact on the Grand Strand in general, and North Myrtle Beach in particular."

Data came from a survey that the S.O.S. conducted. The total population of the ten-question study was 525 attendees at the 2004 Fall Migration. The study revealed some information that underscores the shag's origins in South and North Carolina.

Of the 525 survey respondents, 224 people reported being from North Carolina and 126 reported living in South Carolina. Together these two groups comprised almost 72 percent of the respondents, reinforcing the Carolinas as shag hotbeds, as indeed history proves they are.

Figures at that time from the Myrtle Beach Area Chamber of Commerce reveal that the top five states from which visitors come are North Carolina, New York, Pennsylvania, Ohio, and Virginia. The Fall Migration attracts shaggers, not tourists, as a high proportion of visitors come from the Southeast, shag's predominant region.

One question asked respondents how far they travel to attend the Fall Migration. The 457 who answered this question stated that they traveled at least one hundred miles. Of those, 193 traveled between one hundred and two hundred miles, 130 traveled between two hundred and three hundred miles, and 134 traveled at least three hundred miles.

Another question asked respondents to identify their spending during the Fall Migration. The total amount spent by respondents was approximately $310,000, a weighted average of which was $610.40, a figure higher than the $585 average spending by visitor households in the Grand Strand area as reported by the Myrtle Beach Chamber of Commerce.

One question concerned how long participants stayed for the event. Other questions asked about popular activities pursued while at the beach and what respondents' choices of beverages were at the Fall Migration. As expected more than half of all respondents reported drinking more than one type of adult beverage, which ranged from cocktails to beer and wine.

After all the responses were analyzed, shaggers' economic impact could be boiled down to a succinct summary: "The total amount spent by the 525 individuals who responded to the survey was approximately $310,000." The respondents' average length of stay was 6.49 days, well above the average stay of 4.5 days by other tourists in the Grand Strand area. The total impact depends on the number of visitors attending the Fall Migration. At the time of the survey, the S.O.S. estimate for total Fall Migration attendees was more than 12,000. Math based on statistical procedures reveals that the total direct and indirect spending came to $4.14 million. The event generated an additional $2.61 million, using the Bureau of Economic Analysis expansion multiplier of 0.70, which accounts for the respending of direct and indirect spending in the local economy. The total economic impact came to $6.75 million.

Admittedly the estimate is approximate due to the possibility of sampling biases and statistical errors, but it is merely the tip of the iceberg. Still, the survey reveals some interesting correlations that generally correspond to socio-economic theory.

Those coming from farther away are likely to stay longer and spend more. Those from close by stay in their own residences and spend less. Shaggers staying in condominiums spend less per day and stay longer than those who stay in hotels. The most significant result of the study shows that those who vacation only in North Myrtle Beach during the Fall Migration spend a lot more on average than those who vacation in North Myrtle Beach other times of the year.

The Fall Migration's economic impact on North Myrtle Beach approaches $7 million—a far cry from the days of beach bums with loose change for the Seeburgs, Rock-Olas, and Wurlitzers and the hot dogs and beers. Shaggers appreciate the good times and are quick to share their good fortune with others. In addition they look out for one another now that Father Time has touched many of them with a little thing called age.

The society bought and placed defibrillators in shag haunts where S.O.S. members love to dance. Training, certification, and recertification in the use of defibrillators take place in the O.D. clubs prior to annual S.O.S. Migrations. Beach clubs require designated members of the S.O.S. clubs to undergo three-hour training and hands-on use of the defibrillators.

AN ECONOMIC BOOM

The smooth dance that evolved in the legendary days set in motion a series of events that would create an economic boom for O.D., alas now known as North Myrtle Beach.

Frank Beacham, writing in "Charlie's Place," noted the fact that shaggers and people attentive to the shagging phenomenon found ample ways there to let go of a dollar. He said: "Shagging is big business in Ocean Drive, a small resort community about twenty miles north of where Charlie Fitzgerald's club once stood. On Main Street, Judy's House of Oldies sells hard-to-find beach music records and instructional shag videos, while Beach Memories caters to coastal nostalgia with lithographs, clothing, coffee mugs and bric-a-brac that commemorate legendary South Carolina beach hangouts like the Pad and Roberts Pavilion. Storefront windows display a mountain of shagging kitsch, from T-shirts, cheap watches, and beer bottle covers to specialty ship cruises organized for shag dancers."

Aside from businesses in North Myrtle Beach, some of the shag economy's other, more obvious businesses include the shag clubs and roving deejays who spin beach tunes. In addition art can be included in shagonomics.

Memories—you can make 'em and you can buy 'em in a way. Souvenirs help to recollect the good times. Beacham referred to Beach Memories, an enterprise owned by Becky Stowe. She's made a business out of beach memories, a perfect name for an enterprise that caters to the dance and its nostalgic devotees.

Beach Memories sells official S.O.S. limited-edition prints and beach-themed art, but don't consider Stowe an opportunist. In 1993 she was designated as the Official Artist in Residence for the Society of Stranders. Her artwork preserves shag memories and nostalgia—consider it memorabilia that allow patrons to take bits of shag history back home.

Stowe's shag logo, the one on the North Myrtle Beach water tower, adorns jewelry as well. Much of her merchandise includes wine glasses, shot glasses, and koozies; shaggers love to party, and they have no problem spending money on the good life. Stowe is long familiar with the shag and its followers. Her husband, Milford Powell, owns the Pirate's Cove Lounge in North Myrtle Beach. Shagging is their love and business. And yes, Milford Powell is the same Powell who witnessed the last rites over the Pad's old urinal.

It's telling that Becky Stowe, if not the first, is among the first artists in the United States to commit virtually all of her paintings to the subjects of the beach and shag community. Her pen-and-ink and mixed-media paintings of places such as the original Pad and the Pavilion are memorabilia treasured by many collectors around the world. People other than shaggers are willing to spend money on the shag phenomenon.

In 1987 she created special commemorative, limited-edition prints twice per year for S.O.S. events when more than ten thousand shaggers came to town. Twice a year since 1992, Stowe's art has been featured on the cover of the *Carefree Times*. She received the S.O.S. Chairman's Lifetime Achievement Award in 2000.

Being an artist, Becky Stowe stands out. She is, however, but one of the many people who find in the shag a vocation, a vacation, and a way to help others. Shaggers like to party, and they like to help those in need too. Giving —it's a big part of who they are.

THE SHAG CAUGHT FIRE just after World War II, giving young people an outlet for their restless spirits and an antidote to everyday life. It coincided with a period of prosperity following the war. Then it nearly died during its dark ages, clinging to life in inland pockets and outposts, going through hard times for sure. It pulled through to leave another legacy besides dancing, a fiscal and charitable legacy. The shag's prosperity and then descent into hard times shaped its history and its spirit. Shaggers don't turn away from those experiencing hard times themselves. They've been there.

Today the shag and its cult members play a unique role in the economy and conscience of South and North Carolina. This began when kids dropped change into jukeboxes. It spread and became entrenched in the two states' cultures. It's South Carolina's official state dance and North Carolina's state popular dance.

In 1984 Representative "Bubber" Snow introduced a bill to make the shag South Carolina's official state dance. The S.C. General Assembly by Act No. 329, 1984, designated the shag as the state's official dance. Governor Dick Riley signed the bill into law on April 10, 1984, citing its origin in South Carolina, its revival, and its contribution to the economy, education, and recreation.

Today the shag continues to contribute to the economy in North and South Carolina—not just along the Grand Strand but wherever shag clubs bring people together in the spirit of good times and good causes. Partying and good causes make great partners. Take the "r" and "t" out of "partying," and you get the word "paying." That's apropos, for the Society of Stranders and its members, corporate sponsors, and others pay their dues for membership in another club, a club known as humanity. Shaggers are always ready to help those in need, and the ledger proves it.

(R362, H3591)

AN ACT TO AMEND THE CODE OF LAWS OF SOUTH CAROLINA, 1976, BY ADDING SECTION 1-1-665, SO AS TO DESIGNATE THE SHAG AS THE OFFICIAL DANCE OF THE STATE.

Whereas, all South Carolinians are proud that the shag, one of the great developments in terpsichorean culture, is native to this State, and

Whereas, it is appropriate that the contributions that the shag makes to the cultural life of South Carolina, the United States, and the world should be recognized above all in the birthplace of the shag. Now, therefore,

Be it enacted by the General Assembly of the State of South Carolina:

Shag designated official state dance

SECTION 1. The 1976 Code is amended by adding:
"Section 1-1-665. The shag is the official dance of the State."

Time effective

SECTION 2. This act shall take effect upon approval by the Governor.

In the Senate House the 5th day of April
In the Year of Our Lord One Thousand Nine Hundred and Eighty-Four.

> Michael R. Daniel,
> *President of the Senate*
> W. Sterling Anderson,
> *Speaker Pro Tempore of the*
> *House of Representatives*

Approved the 10th day of April, 1984

> Richard W. Riley,
> Governor

——XX——

To Phil Sawyer —
Great 10th anniversary & Thanks
for the huge success with SOS —
Dick Riley

Printer's Date — 4/13/84 — S.

BE IT ENACTED

Courtesy of Phil Sawyer.

Appendix B

Popular Shag Songs

TOPSONGSOF.COM'S TOP 10 SONGS OF THE 1940S

1. Good Rockin' Tonight by Wynonie Harris
2. Boogie Chillen' by John Lee Hooker
3. Straighten Up and Fly Right by King Cole Trio
4. Who Threw the Whiskey in the Well by Lucky Millinder
5. Blues in the Night by Jimmie Lunceford
6. Too Soon to Know by Orioles
7. Caldonia by Louis Jordan
8. The Honeydripper by Joe Liggins
9. Lovesick Blues by Hank Williams
10. Drinkin' Wine Spo-Dee-O-Dee by Stick McGhee and His Buddies

DigitalDreamdoor.com compiles lists of music favorites created by "knowledgeable people dedicated to the best possible rankings."

THE GLORY YEARS
1950

1. The Fat Man—Fats Domino
2. Please Send Me Someone to Love—Percy Mayfield
3. Teardrops from My Eyes—Ruth Brown
4. Mona Lisa—Nat "King" Cole
5. Tennessee Waltz—Patti Page
6. Long Gone Lonesome Blues—Hank Williams
7. Mardi Gras in New Orleans—Professor Longhair
8. I'm Movin' On—Hank Snow
9. Rollin' Stone—Muddy Waters
10. Double Crossing Blues—Johnny Otis (Little Esther and the Robins)

1951

1. Sixty Minute Man—Dominoes
2. Rocket 88—Jackie Brenston
3. Dust My Broom—Elmore James
4. Cry—Johnnie Ray
5. Too Young—Nat "King" Cole
6. Cold Cold Heart—Hank Williams
7. Glory of Love—Five Keys
8. Three O'Clock Blues—B. B. King
9. Hey Good Lookin'—Hank Williams
10. How High the Moon—Les Paul and Mary Ford

1952

1. Lawdy Miss Clawdy—Lloyd Price
2. Jambalaya (On the Bayou)—Hank Williams
3. Have Mercy Baby—Dominoes
4. One Mint Julep—Clovers
5. Night Train—Jimmy Forrest
6. My Song—Johnny Ace
7. Goin' Home—Fats Domino
8. Moody Mood for Love—King Pleasure
9. Juke—Little Walter
10. Baby, Don't Do It—"5" Royales

1953

1. Money Honey—Drifters featuring Clyde McPhatter
2. Your Cheatin' Heart—Hank Williams
3. Crying in the Chapel—Orioles
4. Gee—Crows
5. Shake a Hand—Faye Adams
6. Honey Hush—Joe Turner
7. Mama, He Treats Your Daughter Mean—Ruth Brown
8. Hound Dog—Willie Mae "Big Mama" Thornton
9. Kaw-Liga—Hank Williams
10. The Things That I Used to Do—Guitar Slim

1954

1. Rock Around the Clock—Bill Haley and His Comets
2. Shake, Rattle and Roll—Joe Turner/Bill Haley and His Comets

3. Earth Angel—Penguins
4. Sh-Boom—Chords
5. That's All Right—Elvis Presley with Scotty and Bill
6. Pledging My Love—Johnny Ace
7. Goodnite Sweetheart Goodnite—Spaniels
8. I've Got a Woman—Ray Charles
9. White Christmas—Drifters featuring Clyde McPhatter
10. Work with Me Annie—Royals/Midnighters

TOP 60 SHAG SONGS BY DIGITAL DREAM

1. Sixty Minute Man—Dominoes
2. Carolina Girls—General Johnson and the Chairmen
3. I Love Beach Music—Embers
4. Ms. Grace—Tymes
5. Summertime's Calling Me—Catalinas
6. Stay—Maurice Williams and the Zodiacs
7. My Girl—Temptations
8. Cool Me Out—Lamont Dozier
9. Under the Boardwalk—Drifters
10. Myrtle Beach Days—Fantastic Shakers
11. Brenda—O. C. Smith
12. One Mint Julep—Clovers
13. It Will Stand—Showmen
14. Rainy Day Bells—Globetrotters
15. Lady Soul—Temptations
16. Be Young, Be Foolish, Be Happy—Tams
17. You're More than a Number in My Little Red Book—Drifters
18. Hey Baby—Bruce Channel
19. With This Ring—Platters
20. Nip Sip—Clovers
21. Party Time Man—Futures
22. Club Savoy—Rockin' Louie and the Mamma Jammers
23. Thank You John—Willie Tee
24. Think—Five Royales
25. (I'm Just Thinking about) Cooling Out—Jerry Butler
26. My Guy—Mary Wells
27. Come Get to This—Marvin Gaye
28. You Bring Out the Boogie in Me—Sonny Terry and Brownie McGhee

29. Hello Stranger—Barbara Lewis
30. 39–21–46—Showmen
31. Green Eyes—Ravens
32. It Ain't No Big Thing—Radiants
33. Work with Me Annie—Midnighters
34. Anna—Arthur Alexander
35. Don't Drop It—Wilbert Harrison
36. It's All Right—Impressions
37. Baby I Need Your Lovin'—Four Tops
38. Good Rockin' Tonight—Wynonie Harris
39. I Got the Fever—Prophets
40. Just a Gigolo/I Ain't Got Nobody—Louis Prima
41. Safronia B—Calvin Boze
42. Going Back to Louisiana—Delbert McClinton
43. Zing Went the Strings of My Heart—Coasters
44. This Old Heart of Mine—Isley Brothers
45. Stubborn Kind of Fellow—Marvin Gaye
46. You're So Fine—Falcons
47. Searchin'—Coasters
48. Drinkin' Wine Spo-Dee-O-Dee—Stick McGhee
49. The Entertainer—Tony Clarke
50. Lipstick Traces—Benny Spellman
51. She Shot a Hole in My Soul—Clifford Curry
52. Give Me Just a Little More Time—Chairmen of the Board
53. Just One Look—Doris Troy
54. But It's Alright—J. J. Jackson
55. What Kind of Fool (Do You Think I Am)—Tams
56. I Need Your Loving—Don Gardner and Dee Dee Ford
57. Easy Comin' Out (Hard Goin' In)—William Bell
58. Girl Watcher—O'Kaysions
59. White Cliffs of Dover—Checkers
60. Annie Had a Baby—Midnighters

TOP SHAG SONGS OF 2010—
ASSOCIATION OF BEACH AND SHAG CLUB DEEJAYS

1. Sweetness of Your Love—L.U.S.T.
2. Why Don't We Just Dance—Josh Turner
3. I Don't Want Nobody—Ike Turner

4. Build Me Up—the Band of Oz
5. Need You Now—Lady Antebellum
6. Let's Walk—Austin de Lone
7. Carina—James Hunter
8. Hip Swingin' Blues—Diedra
9. Stuff You Gotta Watch—Levon Helm
10. An Older Woman—Zac Harmon
11. In This Mess—Snooky Pryor
12. It Only Hurts Me When I Cry—Raul Malo
13. Sign Your Name—Michael Bolton
14. Shame—Mighty Mo Rodgers
15. Dance to the Radio—the Band of Oz
16. Lady Soul—the Temptations
17. 1955—Morry Sochat and the Special 20's
18. I Used to Cry Mercy Mercy—the Lamplighters
19. The Bop—Ms. Jody
20. Dirty O' Man—the Hardway Connection
21. One Night Stand—Andre Lee
22. Doot Dootsie Wah—Little Isidore
23. How Do You Stop—James Brown
24. Mama's Drinkin' Liquor Again—King Tyrone and the Graveyard Ramblers
25. Impossible—the Craig Woolard Band
26. Just Go—Lionel Richie and Akon
27. Stuck on You—3T
28. Jukebox—the Holiday Band
29. Nine One One—the R & B Bombers
30. Boardwalk—Angel Goldrush and Jerry Shooter
31. Come Get to This—Marvin Gaye
32. No More Cloudy Days—the Eagles
33. I Can't Think—the Band of Oz
34. You Can't Win—James Hunter
35. Just Your Fool—Cyndi Lauper and Charlie Misselwhite
36. Bright—Peter White
37. Hold on to the Blues—Lonnie Givens
38. Katrina, Katrina—Henry Gray
39. Too Much Booty Shakin' (Up in Here)—Jonathan Burton
40. Getaway Car—Hall and Oates
41. Touching in the Dark—Rhonda McDaniel

42. My Big Sister's Radio—the Mighty Mike Schermer Band
43. Lover, Lover—Mark Roberts and Breeze
44. Cry to Me—Solomon Burke
45. 8–3–1—Lisa Stansfield
46. Eyes on You—the Hardway Connection
47. Give Me You—Billy Ward and the Dominoes
48. Your Love Is Amazing—the Craig Woolard Band
49. Ready to Dance the Night Away—Diedra
50. Mama Didn't Know—Frederick Mangum

Index

About the authors

PHIL SAWYER earned his undergraduate and graduate degrees and his Ph.D. from the University of South Carolina. A native of Salley, South Carolina, Sawyer is a U.S. Army veteran and retired educator. An integral part of the shag movement, Sawyer serves as president emeritus of the Society of Stranders and was honored with its Lifetime Achievement award in 2011.

TOM POLAND is a native of Georgia and a University of Georgia graduate. He has published six books, three of which were collaborations with Robert C. Clark and published by the University of South Carolina Press, including *Reflections of South Carolina.*